TRAIN SHUNTING AND MARSHALLING

for the Modeller

TRAIN SHUNTING AND MARSHALLING

for the Modeller

BOB ESSERY

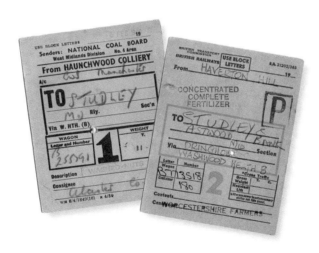

Ian Allan

PUBLISHING

First published 2011

ISBN 978 0 7110 3632 1

Published by Ian Allan Publishing
an imprint of Ian Allan Publishing Ltd, Hersham,
Surrey, KT12 4RG

Printed in England by Ian Allan Printing Ltd,
Hersham, Surrey, KT12 4RG

Distributed in the United States of America and
Canada by BookMasters Distribution Services

Visit the Ian Allan Publishing website at
www.ianallanpublishing.com

ABOVE The most common method of flat shunting was
for the shunt engine to draw a number (or 'string') of
wagons along a shunting neck and follow the signals
from the shunter. The driver would propel them towards
the sidings. In addition to the shunter uncoupling the
wagons, other shunters set the hand points and pinned
down brakes; all the above activity can be seen in this
picture, taken at the old Midland yard at Wellingborough
on 5 April 1894. At this time wagons generally had only
one brake hand lever; note that neither the wagon
closest to the camera nor the one to the left have
visible levers, while the one in the centre of the picture
has a shunter applying the handbrake as it runs into
the siding.

PAGE 2 The Birmingham West pilot spent a lot of time
doing nothing. It was there to assist any overloaded
westbound trains by providing banking assistance
through the tunnels towards Five Ways and, if required,
to work through to Gloucester as an assisting engine
coupled in front of the train engine. It also did all the
shunting at the west end of the Midland side of the
station, including shunting the Fish sidings to the right
of the picture where the passenger brakevans are
standing. It was always a passenger tender engine and
a Class 2P 4-4-0 was normally provided for these duties.
M. Mensing

Contents

Acknowledgements

Thanks to Andy McMillan for suggesting shunting as the subject of a book, and for reading and commenting upon it; to Emma Haywood for writing the foreword; to Steve Banks, Roger Carpenter, John Edgington, Peter Tatlow and Peter Waller, for their help in sourcing photographs; to John Copsey for his advice on railway terms, in particular those applicable to the old GWR. And finally to Steve Banks – for his useful overall comments about the contents – and Tony Overton – for reading the text and making a number of suggestions, some based upon his personal experience.

Bob Essery
BEDWORTH, WARWICKSHIRE, 2011

Foreword

Improvements in materials and processes over the years have increased the quality of both ready-to-run and kit-built/scratch-built model railway rolling stock in leaps and bounds. Many current model layouts have rolling stock and scenery that would previously only have been seen behind a museum showcase, some 50 or so years ago. The popularity of the four earlier books in the 'For the Modeller' series has demonstrated a growing interest in the prototypical engineering and operation of their model railway layout, to compliment the rolling stock and scenery.

Although today's railway – with its multiple-unit operation and its multitude of colour light signals – seems a far cry from the early 20th century's age of steam, many of the current signalling, engineering and operating practices can still trace their heritage back to those times and the earlier Regulation of the Railways Act (1889) – otherwise known as the 'Lock, Block and Brake Act'. While the traditional mechanical signalbox, with its semaphore signals, is slowly being replaced by centralised signalling control centres with colour light signals and advances are being made in in-cab signalling, the underlying purpose of the 1889 act still holds true – to keep trains safely spaced apart whilst travelling as fast as possible, for the safety and comfort of passengers.

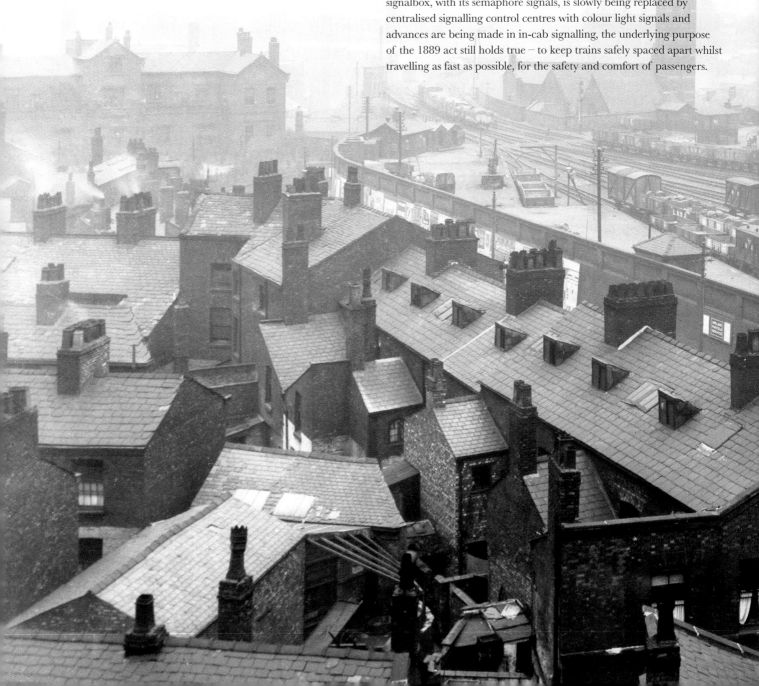

Not all prototypical situations and rules can be successfully applied to a model railway, but building and operating a layout by studying and researching its prototype can be both enjoyable to the modeller and entertainingly educational to the public at exhibitions. Bob Essery is well known for his attention to detail in the operation of railways and this series of books underlines his commitment and enthusiasm for authenticity which, if not attained, can sometimes spoil what should be a first-class layout.

The railway has some 200 years of engineering and operating history covering many individual subjects. This series has touched on some of them, and I hope that railway modellers reading this book will find inspiration that they can translate to their own layout.

Emma Haywood

CRANBERRY, STAFFORDSHIRE, 2011

Emma Haywood has some 35 years' experience as a signalling design engineer across the UK railway network and currently manages a signalling design office for the country's leading railway infrastructure companies. She is also an active railway modeller in Scale 7.

BELOW This picture was taken on 15 May 1922 at Manchester Ancoats. At first sight this is a mass of wagons on sidings, but careful examination shows they have been shunted into some order. Close to the camera we can see a couple of brakevans and a line of wagons loaded with barrels. The three vans on the siding close to the wall are a pair of meat vans and a ventilated van with a few low-sided open wagons. Note the number of goods wagons with their doors open, waiting to be shunted into the shed for loading. There is also a line of open goods wagons waiting for their loads and most, if not all of them, have been shunted in readiness.

The picture was taken a few months before the 1923 grouping, but after the common user agreements for certain wagon types were in place. As such, it presents a more colourful scene than would be seen in ten years' time. Also note the back-to-back terrace housing which, together with factories, was a feature of the inner cities that often surrounded the railway infrastructure.

Introduction

When I was about 12 years of age, my parents and I lived in the Small Heath district of Birmingham not far from Small Heath and Sparkbrook station, which was at the south end of the marshalling sidings at Bordesley on the GWR London to Wolverhampton line. The station was within easy walking distance from my home and I spent many hours watching the trains pass below the road bridge, which was our vantage point. Although the prime object was to note the numbers of the locomotives passing by, I also watched and wondered at what was happening.

Later, I began to go on organised visits to locomotive sheds, but while I wanted to look at all aspects of the depot it seemed to me that I was the odd man out. All the others wanted was to note all the engine numbers and move on to the next shed as quickly as possible, but to me there was a fascination about how the railway system operated which went far beyond simply number-taking. A few years later, I started work on the railway at Saltley; although it was only for a few years, I like to think that this was part of a lifetime of research – research which was in turn translated into modelling – which has given me a good insight into how it was done.

Although this is not the place to relate my modelling activity since I first began it in 1946, I should emphasise that most of my

efforts have been directed towards achieving what I describe as 'realism in miniature', an attempt to reproduce in model form what happened on the prototype. When I began, two-rail electrification on model railways was in its infancy and clockwork was commonplace, but over the years all this has changed. Today's modeller has (with apologies to Harold Macmillan) never had it so good.

On the other side of the coin, we have the modeller's understanding of how the traditional steam railway was operated. As I have said on a number of occasions: over the years, for every improvement in materials, methods and models that has taken place, there has been a corresponding decline in the modeller's understanding of how the steam railway was operated. However, we cannot

blame the modeller; other than the preserved railways where freight traffic is almost non-existent, he can no longer watch a steam railway at work. Nor has much space been devoted to the subject of railway operation within the vast amount of railway literature that has been published.

Modellers tend to copy other modellers and so errors multiply. It was with these thoughts in mind that the idea for a book to set out the broad principles of railway operating practice during the steam era was born, during a conversation with Peter Waller of Ian Allan Publishing. We also agreed that, if *Railway Operation for the Modeller* was successful, we could add additional titles that would cover in greater detail certain aspects of railway operation, and so a series was born.

LEFT Tunnel Hill Junction, Worcester, 1959. Note the old GWR Worcester Goods Yard to the left, the locomotive works in the centre and the motive power depot on the far right. As a 2-8-0 No 2845 with a South Wales-to-Bordesley freight train is taking water, a '2251' class 0-6-0 No 2221 heads a freight train for Oxley. Both are waiting for the express passenger train headed by a BR Standard Class 5 No 73155 to clear the block section before one of them can proceed. There is a GWR pannier tank in the yard and another unidentified engine close to the works. Yards where shunting took place were often close to locomotive sheds and passenger stations; this aspect of the prototype is helpful for space-starved modellers. *T. A. C. Radway*

We continued with *Passenger Train Operation* and followed this with *Freight Train Operation*; next came *Railway Signalling and Track Plans*, and now this fifth volume covers shunting and train marshalling – a highly involved subject that includes aspects which have been featured in the first four titles. However, I have tried to blend the mixture so that the series can be viewed as five parts of one all-embracing title. To avoid unnecessary duplication, therefore, there are a number of cross-references to the earlier parts of the series, given in the hope that modellers will see this series as a must-have when designing, building and operating their own version of 'realism in miniature'.

In my view, the hobby of model railways is wide-ranging and absorbing. There are so many facets which can become captivating and sidetrack a modeller into one particular aspect, and so it is useful to develop a clear idea of what you want to create. Modellers have a variety of options open to them, ranging from just wanting to see trains run by to operating highly complex systems. At times I find myself in discussion with modellers who appear to believe the methods used by 'their' railway company are different from those of the others, and that what applied years ago is not applicable today. (However, I hope these views have been answered by Emma Haywood in the Foreword.)

I also often encounter the belief that the future lies with the post-steam era and in particular what can be seen today. I take a different view. While I agree that the future health of the hobby depends on attracting younger modellers, I do not agree they are only interested in what is often referred to as 'modern image'. On more than one occasion I have found junior modellers most receptive to proper operating procedures and the fact that the models in use represent, in my case, the Edwardian era is of no account. It is a railway and they are operating it correctly. Nor is the enjoyment confined to youngsters. On more than one occasion within our group I've heard comment that there is a lot of fun to be had when you operate correctly, regardless of the period being modelled. Indeed, from a personal standpoint, my enjoyment and satisfaction stem from the knowledge that a subject has been properly researched. Where

ABOVE Chilwell sidings, Toton, 14 February 1910. Note the way the sidings have been set out to run parallel to each other and the use of three throw turnouts to obtain the maximum length of siding within the space available. To assist the shunters, the rodding to the switchblades from the point levers for the centre fan of three sidings has been taken below the gathering line on the right.

possible, my findings have been made available to others – so that models based upon that research will represent, as near as possible, *reality in miniature*.

Railway terms and their meanings

During the preparation of this book, it became very clear that the meaning of certain words varied; some ex-railwaymen had a slightly different understanding of the same word to modern railway authors. This became very clear when consulting railway operating books written by serving railwaymen during the early 20th century. In writing this book, I have attempted to reach a consensus while at the same time recognising that some readers may query my findings. However, I would point out that most modern-day railway enthusiasts (in particular modellers) will describe a piece of pointwork as a 'frog,' but the correct British railway description (and the one I use) is 'common crossing'. A Glossary of Terms that covers both shunting and marshalling supplements that found in *Railway Operation for the Modeller* has been included at page 94.

LEFT Sidings full of loaded coal wagons were typical of British railways during the steam era and beyond, although the impact of North Sea gas and the use of oil saw a marked reduction of this traffic. Photographed at Cricklewood in 1905, the absence of private owner wagons suggests this may be locomotive coal for use at the company's London engine sheds.

The word 'shunt' has a variety of meanings in the railway world; thus, a freight train en route may be shunted into a refuge siding to permit a more important train to pass; a passenger train after arrival at a station may be shunted to a bay line or a siding. Then there is also the shunting of wagons (or coaches) as distinct from trains, and here again the word covers a variety of operations. An arriving train is broken up, or marshalled; a siding is shunted, wagons ready for away being shunted out and those not ready being put back. Other forms of shunting include placing wagons in position for different operations, under a crane or into a dock, or some other internal work that has no direct connection with train working.

The above words were written by E. D. Gilmour and appeared in the June 1961 edition of *Model Railway News*. It should be pointed out that Gilmour was a railwayman who held the position of yardmaster; therefore he was well placed to know the correct terms.

The most difficult part of this book has been finding the pictures to illustrate the variety of features that fall under the heading of shunting and train marshalling, without duplicating what has been used in other titles in the series. As we will see, period is of less importance, so I have used the best pictures I can find to illustrate the subject without worrying if they were taken in 1900 or the 1960s. Although I have tried to include as many different companies as I can, it should be pointed out that (while there would be local practices) there was not much variation from

company to company. Broadly speaking, after 1923 the rulebook for each was very similar.

Therefore, if your interests are in the XYZ Railway and we have featured the ABC Railway, rest assured that their overall methods for shunting and train marshalling would not differ very much. The one company that tended to differ from the rest was the GWR; examples of where GWR practice was at variance with other railway companies are noted in both this and the previous titles in the series.

ABOVE This picture was taken at Bristol St Philips Goods Station Yard on 30 May 1922 and demonstrates the almost timeless nature of the steam railway. The locomotive, a Midland Railway 0-6-0T, could have been seen there 20 years before and a few of the class were still in service in 1960. During this period the work of shunting was largely unaltered, although by 1960 many sources of freight traffic were now using other means of transport. *NRM DY 12624*

RIGHT Compare this picture, taken at Pratts sidings on the North Staffordshire Railway *circa* the late 1880s, with the picture below. More than 60 years separate them, but the most obvious difference is that the British Railways uniforms are smarter. Here the enginemen have joined the guard and two shunters to form a group who, together with the signalman (still in his box), will shunt and marshal the trains.

LEFT 'Right away' is the message conveyed to the driver by this GWR guard on the veranda of his brakevan. Although a posed picture, it shows how the signal was given. Until it was received, the driver would not start his engine. *Ian Allan Library*

OPPOSITE LEFT This delightful picture, taken during the post-1948 period, shows the driver of Class 4F No 44403 with two traffic department staff members – probably a traffic inspector on the left and a goods guard to the right, though the latter could also be a shunter.

OPPOSITE RIGHT When this book was in preparation, many modellers expressed surprise when I said capstans remained in use until the end of steam. This picture was taken on 26 June 1964, when I was at Heaton Mersey; the wagon inside the warehouse on the left is attached to the rope that runs across the picture.

1 The evolution of shunting

At the beginning of the railway age, shunting – in other words the movement of wagons from one line to another by a locomotive, either singly or coupled together – was probably rather rare. At this time rail wagons were light and could be moved by hand, so it is probable that the short-distance movement of wagons from A to B was undertaken via pinch bars, horses, capstans or simply by pushing them a short distance – a practice I observed still in use during the 1950s. Wagon turntables, used to move wagons from one set of lines to another, were also employed to shunt coaches in a similar manner. The practice ceased when the vehicles increased in size and the coaches' wheelbases could not be accommodated on the turntables. However, this did not apply to wagons and wagon turntables, which were usually found at warehouses and goods sheds and continued to be used until the final years of steam.

During the early years of the Victorian steam railway, the absence of an efficient braking system made shunting by a steam locomotive, as we understand it today, virtually impossible. All that was available to the driver was a handbrake applied by the fireman, but the size and weight of all rolling stock was far less than after the late 1890s. Steam braking on locomotives used for shunting dates from c1870; before then, most shunting was probably accomplished by using horses.

To make this point, I feel we should begin with a description of how things were done in the mid-1880s by quoting from the *Railways of England* by W. M. Ackworth, which illustrates how shunting was undertaken at two of the Midland Railway's major marshalling sidings – Chaddesden near Derby and Toton on the Erewash Valley line:

A train arrives, its engine is uncoupled, and a second or shunting engine is attached at the back. This engine then pushes the train forward to a shunting neck, which opens out to no less than 35 lines. The couplings between the separate shunts, single trucks or sets of trucks are unhooked; to each shunt one or more horses are attached, and the trucks are by them drawn forward into their appointed sidings. A train of 40 trucks is in this way broken up in from three and a half to four and a half minutes.

Ackworth also states that at Chaddesden there were six engines and between 50 and 100 horses at work, while there were 50 horses stabled at Toton. As we can see in this description from the 1880s, the locomotive did not shunt the wagons; horses did. How it was done at other locations such as small goods yards is open to conjecture; apart from

LEFT This 19th-century picture (no specific date given) was taken somewhere on the North Staffordshire Railway and shows the arrangements for horse shunting. The horse is attached to the wagon by a chain, which is part of its harness, and has a hook attached to the wagon coupling hook.

Ackworth, as quoted above, there appears to have been very little – if anything – recorded about shunting during this period. My assumption is that a resident shunting horse, or the train engine, did the shunting.

Over the years the balance changed. After the 1880s, the increase in wagon size and weight, together with a vast increase in traffic, made the use of horses as the main motive power in large shunting yards impractical. With the advent of steam brakes as standard fittings locomotives began to take over from horses, which were used only when it was not practical to use any other source of power. However, as we will see later in a section describing work at Camden Yard, there was still a traditional reliance on wagon turntables and, to a lesser degree, traversers to marshal goods wagons. This practice continued across the British railway system until the final years of steam.

However little may have been written about shunting wagons, it is still far more than exists about coaches. I can only assume that, until the wheelbases became too long, turntables were used at stations and carriage sidings, but when this was no longer possible they were shunted by capstans and horses, with locomotives employed when they were available or booked to undertake the work.

However, with the increase in size and weight of coaches, locomotives became the preferred method for shunting carriages.

Many of the British railway companies did not really make extensive use of specialised shunting locomotives, except at some locations on the system – such as docks, breweries, collieries, etc – where small, short wheelbase engines were required due to restricted clearances, lightly laid track or sharp curves. Instead, they employed whatever suitable motive power was available.

For many years, tender locomotives were just as likely to be employed for dedicated

ABOVE This picture was taken at the Midland Railway creosote works at Beeston, where sleepers were prepared for use. Here we see a shunting horse moving loads of sleepers over the works system. It was no doubt also used to move the wagons that brought sleepers for creosoting and took them away to where they were to be stored.

shunting duties as tank engines. The mid-1920 minutes of the LMS company's traffic committee refer to the need to build more shunting tank engines, instead of using tender engines for shunting work. However, while the production of more 0-6-0 tanks released tender engines for other duties, train engines (usually tender locomotives) were often employed for shunting purposes as part of their diagrammed work. Modellers should be selective in their use of dedicated shunting engines, as often the use of a train engine will be more realistic. However, there were good

LEFT Wagon turntables played an important part in the shunting and marshalling of freight stock both in goods sheds and in the open yard. This interior view of Leicester LNWR shed was taken in 1922. It shows how it was possible to move wagons along one line and then to remove them by placing them onto the turntable and turning it, so that they could be drawn away along another line. Note the capstan and bollards used to draw the wagons through the shed.

Each table was fitted with a suitable number of hinged stop keys to stop the turntable as required and bring the lines of the table into alignment with those to which the vehicle was to be transferred. The 'hooker-on' (capstan man's assistant) turned the stop key so that, when the table was aligned, the key engaged a slot in the rim of the turntable pit and arrested the movement. The transfer of the vehicle between the table and the siding or reverse was then made.

reasons why tank engines were usually preferable to tender engines for shunting work – such as better rearward visibility, reduced length and better adhesion for a given size, a subject we explore in greater detail in Chapter 6, where we examine the types of locomotives used for shunting.

Unlike in *The Oxford English Dictionary*, the word 'shunt' has many meanings to railwaymen. To supplement what appears in the Glossary, I have set out the 'moves' – to use a railway expression – that describe the many different physical acts of shunting freight and passenger stock to marshal it into the required train formation:

- To assemble two or more vehicles in order to make up a train.
- To add vehicles to an existing train.
- To break up a train and to place the vehicles onto other lines.
- To detach one or more vehicles from a train.
- To reposition vehicles for loading or unloading – for example, to move empty wagons from a siding into a goods shed
- To load, or to move loaded wagons away, from a goods shed prior to their being made into a train.
- The movement of empty loco coal wagons away from a coaling stage, to replace them with loaded ones.
- To detach or attach vehicles to passenger trains while at a station – i.e. horseboxes, parcels vans, additional carriages or dining cars – or the division of one train, or the forming of one train out of two, ready for departure.
- To move dead engines, or those with insufficient boiler pressure to run under their own steam.
- To move entire trains from one running line to another, or into a siding or lay-by, to enable another train to overtake.

- To move the carriages of a passenger train from the arrival platform into a departure platform, bay platform line or siding.

ABOVE Capstans were widely used in the open yard. Here we see a Great Central open wagon being turned by a capstan; the hook at the end of the chain was attached to the wagon axleguard and the movement was controlled by the capstan man.

Couplings

Couplings attach vehicles to one another. The number of links has varied over the years; early couplings could have as many as five links or more, but later three-link couplings became the standard. A variation of the three-link was the Instanter coupling, which had the central one of its three links in the shape of an isosceles triangle (two long sides and one short one). By rotating the central link to take the pull using its short side, it was possible to reduce the amount of slack between the wagons and thus reduce the chance of a breakaway from oscillation. It was heavier than a three-link coupling, but a skilled man could couple them with a shunting pole and then, by using his pole with the buffer-stock as a fulcrum, flick the single end down to engage the short link.

In addition, there were also screw couplings commonly used only on passenger and non-passenger coaching stock or, later, on most 'fitted' goods stock. The latter entailed a man having to go between vehicles to turn a toggle tightening the two screws on either end of the coupling; because they were opposite threads, it pulled the outer links closer. The man doing the coupling also had to perform other necessary work, including connecting the brake vacuum pipes and – if it was coaching stock during the steam heating season – the carriage-warming pipes. Although not part of the process of shunting, the separation or coupling of carriages could also involve corridor connections. During the 19th century, safety chains were used while cords or fine chains – for the passenger alarm-pulls and auto-train controls that were part of some systems – also had to be connected. Finally, we must not overlook the buckeye coupling: a semi-automatic system which only required vehicles to be pushed together in order to couple them, although the through pipes still had to be coupled manually.

Shunting was carried out almost anywhere but mostly involved goods traffic in marshalling

LEFT The size of the hump used for gravity shunting varied; this example, photographed at Nuneaton on 26 June 1931, illustrates a LNWR 'Super D' 0-8-0 shunting wagons over a small hump. *H. N. James*

yards, where trains were assembled or broken up, or at smaller goods yards, usually close to the passenger station where the wagons took on their cargoes or were offloaded. Much of this shunting was carried out by the train engine and is typical of that seen on many model railways. With carriage stock one cannot be so specific. After carriages became too long to be shunted on turntables, the work of shunting them was largely confined to carriage siding and passenger stations; carriages tended to be retained in sets, which were strengthened or reduced as and when required. The strengthening vehicles could be one or more carriages. (We examine the complex story of passenger stock in Chapter 3.)

If we consider marshalling yards – or the sidings where wagons were shunted – then there were basically three methods: 'gravitation', 'hump' and 'flat'. Probably the least common was gravitation, where the sidings were laid out on land with a distinct falling gradient to enable individual wagons, once released, to freewheel into the desired siding. Shunting by gravitation was employed from early on in railway history, in particular for coaling ships on the Tyne and for sorting mineral trains at Darlington on the old North Eastern Railway; there were also others, with the LNWR Edge Hill Gravity Gridiron (its first portion constructed in 1875) probably being the best known.

Many Welsh coalmines on steeply graded lines used gravitation to drop wagons from reception sidings under their chutes for loading, and then again to drop them into departure sidings. Hump shunting was not too dissimilar, but was more commonly used; the wagons were pushed on a rising gradient over a hump and the falling gradient on the other side gave the vehicles enough momentum to roll into the required siding. However, flat shunting was the most common system – which is just as well as far as modelling is concerned. The other two would almost certainly need some form of motorised rolling stock to simulate any degree of realism, especially in the smaller gauges.

On the full-size railway, it is probably true to say that no two yards were alike. There were differences in gradients, the number of wagons that could be accommodated, traffic-flow rates and the general layout of the yard, as well as the traffic requirements. These all had a bearing upon how the yard could be shunted. At some yards the gradients fell slightly towards the buffer stops, which allowed gravity to help the wagons roll into the sidings, but the majority of them were flat. The shunting engine drew

ABOVE This picture was taken at Whitemoor on the old Great Eastern Railway, to the east of Peterborough; it shows one of the major LNER marshalling yards. Note how the wagons rolled towards the sidings; the points were operated from the control cabin whose staff could also reduce the speed of the wagons as they came down the hill by activating the retarder. *NRM SX 536*

LEFT The interior of the control tower for the Down Yard sidings at Toton, photographed on 27 July 1939. *NRM DY 26068*

ABOVE The location of this picture is uncertain, but it shows a loading gauge that measured the loads being carried. These were a feature of most goods stations. It was necessary for some loaded wagons to be either drawn or propelled under them to check that they were 'within gauge'. *Ian Allan Library*

ABOVE Unlike hump shunting, it is possible to reproduce shunting wagons via a wagon hoist on a model railway. This picture was taken at Leytonstone in 1909, but the method of lifting wagons could still be seen 50 years later. The wagon hoist comprised a platform onto which the wagon was run. The man in charge – who could be a hoist or capstan man – controlled the up or down movement using the automatic gear which was hydraulic or electric powered. The most usual method was to use hydraulic rams, although there was also the balanced type which comprised two platforms, one on each side of the line, that moved up and down at the same time.

ABOVE AND LEFT Our first two pictures were taken at the Cambridge Street St Pancras coal drops in March 1905. The first move was to bring the loaded coal wagons forward to the end of the siding, at right angles to the line that took the wagon to where the coal was dropped into the cart. Then the wagon was moved onto the traverser, which can be seen in both pictures – far left of picture one, centre of platform in picture two. A shunting horse was attached to the wagon, which was drawn along the rails to the coal drop where the wagon's bottom doors were opened and it was emptied. It was then drawn back to a siding to begin its return journey to the colliery. This method of moving wagons was also used in goods sheds; our third picture illustrates how a traverser was attached to the capstan and brought the wagon to the side of the deck from the siding on the right of the picture.

BELOW These illustrations were taken from a British Railways booklet entitled *Your Personal Safety*. They have been included to show the use of 'pinch bars', referred to here as wagon levers, which probably continued up to and beyond the end of steam, as did the practice of pushing wagons a short distance.

(b) Movement of individual wagons

Use the proper wagon lever, don't use unauthorised gear.

IT'S "EASY" IF THE TRIANGULAR STEEL BIT IS SHARP (SEE INSET).
"SHARP'S THE WORD, THEN QUICK'S THE ACTION"

8

Always push at *rear* of wagon; watch out for any rebound and for wagons creeping up behind.

Be prepared to apply the brake instantly, but don't rely on brake alone on gradients; use a wagon scotch.

Couple and uncouple by means of the shunting pole and don't ride on this, otherwise it may lead to a different "ride" in an ambulance.

Don't try to squeeze between a structure and a wagon unless you are absolutely certain there will be no movement.

NOT THE PLACE TO "SQUEEZE" IN

9

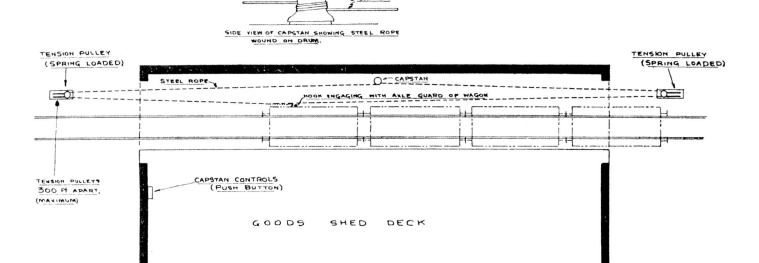

ABOVE Shunting wagons in goods sheds was not easy. In a small shed they could be moved via the use of 'reach wagons' coupled to both the engine and the wagon; these ensured the locomotive did not enter the shed, but in medium and large sheds capstans were employed. One method was to use loop capstans, as this drawing shows. Hooks attached to a lengthy steel rope were hooked onto wagon axleguards and the capstan moved the wagons through the shed.

a 'string' or 'raft' of wagons into the shunting neck and, once the last vehicle was clear of the furthest set of points, the points for the first siding would be set, the first wagons uncoupled and the engine would accelerate forward; the wagons rolled towards the siding and the engine stopped. If necessary, wagons were given additional acceleration by 'hitting up': the points were set for the next shunt and so on, until all the wagons were in the allocated sidings. This method reduced the amount of times the engine would be reversed and the vehicles drawn back along the shunting neck.

Many sidings were built on level ground and, while the process described above for downhill-sloping sidings can be used, it will not be so effective and more reversals will be required. Perfectly flat sidings laid with the aid of a spirit level are the only ones really suitable for modellers; the freer the bearings the more wagons your engines can pull, but without brakes they are more likely to run into any depressions – including those not immediately visible to the naked eye. I suggest you test your sidings with a few very free-running wagons before ballasting them.

In addition to the types of yard mentioned above, sidings were either single- or double-ended, allowing trains to depart from either end. Operationally, double-ended was better because it could be shunted from both ends, but with a single-ended yard all the shunting was done from the exit end. To assist modellers designing a shunting yard, I have extracted some comments from *Railway Permanent Way* by William Heyworth and J. Thomas Lee which I hope will be helpful:

When designing a new siding layout the general lay-out will be determined by the shape and space available and the object may be to have as much siding standing room as possible, regardless of regular or ideal alignment of the tracks. If this is the case there are still some rules that apply and these will be given later. On the other hand space available may allow the sidings to be designed to allow easy running on all routes, using curves of a constant radius wherever possible giving the maximum amount of standing room obtainable, compatible with the requirement of easy running. If the main lines and the sidings parallel thereto are on the curve, it will usually be found that the gathering line should have the same curve, and the same angle between it and the main as with straight tracks in a similar design.

Examples of track layouts will be found in *Railway Signalling and Track Plans*. The Board of Trade Requirements state that 'safety points' must be provided upon goods lines and sidings at their junctions with passenger lines, a feature that is often overlooked by many modellers. These catch and trap points are intended to prevent vehicles running from the sidings onto, or foul of, the main line without permission of the signalman.

Without doubt, the various railways rulebooks give the best insight into the 'do's' and 'don'ts' of prototypical shunting during the periods followed by most modellers. Extracts follow below from the LMS edition of 1933, which was reprinted in 1939 and is very similar to the rulebooks issued by the LNER, GWR and Southern and the later British Railway rulebook:

- During shunting operations drivers must work only to signals given by the guard, shunter or other person in charge, and a driver must not move his train until he has received such a signal, although the fixed signal may have been lowered. The person giving the signals must do so in such a way as to avoid the signals being taken by any driver other than the one for whom they are intended. Should the driver lose sight of the shunter he should stop.
- Double shunting… the rulebook makes it clear experienced men must only carry out this movement.
- Vehicles must not be loose shunted, i.e. without remaining attached to the engine, into sidings or upon running lines unless, where necessary, they are accompanied a sufficient distance by a competent person prepared to apply the hand brakes or sprags to ensure the vehicles being brought to a stand at the required place, or to prevent them coming into violent contact with other vehicles, or the buffer stops, or fouling other lines.
- Loose shunting of any vehicles, by engines, against loaded passenger vehicles (also loose

shunting, by engines, of vehicles containing passengers or explosives) is strictly prohibited.

- Loose shunting, by engines, of vehicles containing livestock should be avoided as far as possible, but may be adopted when absolutely necessary, provided the brake is in good order, and the guard or shunter controls the movement.

- Loose shunting of vehicles into loading docks, stages, warehouse platforms etc is prohibited unless the brakes can be applied without risk of injury to the men operating them.

- The movement of vehicles by means of a prop or pole, or by towing with a rope or chain attached to an engine or vehicle moving on an adjacent line, is strictly prohibited, except where specially authorised by the Chief Operating Manager. [We will examine this method of shunting later in Chapter 4, an arrangement that can be reproduced in model form.]

- Vehicles standing in sidings must be properly secured and left sufficiently clear of the fouling points of any adjoining sidings or lines, to admit of anyone engaged in shunting operations passing safely between such vehicles and any vehicles that may be standing or are being shunted on adjoining sidings or lines. Modellers should thus note that filling any siding to the point where shunting the one next to it would only just miss the last vehicle would have been considered 'unsafe practice', and will always appear wrong to the knowledgeable.

- After the operations are completed, trains or vehicles are to be left inside and clear of any running lines and within trap points, derailers, or scotch blocks; that points not worked from a signalbox are in their normal position; that scotch blocks, where provided are placed across the rails; and no vehicle is left inadvertently upon any running line.

- Vehicles loaded with long timber or other long articles secured by chains or ropes and stanchions upon more than two wagons must not be shunted when a passenger train is passing or signalled to approach if the line on which the passenger train travels would be at all likely to become fouled should the wagons leave the rails. Guards, shunters, signalmen and others concerned must come to a proper understanding when necessary to stop the shunting of such vehicles.

- When vehicles are detached and left on any running line, the signalman must be at once informed in order that he may keep the necessary signals at danger and take the proper steps for securing safety.

- When it is necessary for a train or vehicle to be placed outside a home signal, this must not be done without the signalman's permission and, unless specially authorised, no train without a brake van in rear or vehicle on which the brake cannot be firmly secured must be placed outside a home signal where the line is on a falling gradient towards the signalbox in rear.

- Vehicles must, when practicable, be attached to or detached from a passenger train without the train being moved.

- Whenever it is necessary at stations where absolute block working is in force for an engine to be brought to the rear of a train for the purpose of attaching or detaching vehicles, or removing from the section vehicles which have been detached from a train which has gone forward, the operation must only be carried out after the driver has been clearly verbally instructed by the person in charge what movement is to be made. The driver may, if necessary, be instructed to pass a signal at danger for the purpose.

- The standard code of audible signals by means of bell, gong, horn, whistle, or other appliance used for signalling to drivers engaged in shunting operations is as follows:

Signal	Indicates
One	Go ahead
Two	Set back
Three	Stop
Four	Ease couplings

In order to set out how freight traffic was handled in the United Kingdom, I felt it would be useful to paraphrase an article that was published in the *LMS Magazine*, which described handling rail traffic at Camden Yard. Although this was one of several major goods stations in London, it should be noted that the bulk of goods traffic in the United Kingdom was between the major centres of population where it was not unusual for a railway company to have more than one depot. As a young, inquisitive fireman, I recall asking my driver why there were so many ex-LMS goods stations in the Birmingham area and not just one very big one. His answer was simple – 'It has always been like that.' – but later I realised the growth of traffic had added more track to the original yard, growing in a somewhat arbitrary manner. The result was not an efficient layout, but in many respects this is helpful to space-starved modellers!

The 1923 grouping (the 'Great Amalgamation') saw what had been separate companies' goods facilities become part of the

RIGHT Toton, 31 July 1939. This picture demonstrates how a modern hump-shunting installation is operated. The wagons are propelled up a rising gradient towards the hump. The groups of wagons are uncoupled and pushed over the hump; thereafter, gravity ensures they run forward into the siding. Braking is administered at the control tower and coloured light signals advise the driver of the shunt engine what action to take. The precise arrangements vary from yard to yard, but the principles of hump shunting are universal. *Ian Allan Library*

CENTRE LEFT Petrol-driven shunting tractors were employed at goods stations where there was a requirement for low-capacity shunting power. Rubber-tyred road tractors were adapted for this purpose, equipped with either buffers or a headstock as seen here. Many had draw hooks and short wire cables for towing goods stock. *Michael Andress*

CENTRE RIGHT During the late 1950s and 1960s, attempts to improve and modernise the movement of freight and mineral traffic were made, including the construction of new marshalling yards. This picture shows the New Tees marshalling yard that opened on 21 May 1963 and illustrates cuts of wagons running from the down yard hump. The control room can be seen at the crest of the hump. *British Railways*

BOTTOM LEFT The work of modernising all aspects of goods traffic really got underway during the 1930s. Aided by cheap government loans, improvements in handling the loading and unloading of traffic began with the object of reducing costs and speeding up movement. World War Two largely brought this to an end but, as British Railways sought to reduce their operating deficit, modernisation schemes were implemented – sadly to little avail. By the late 1950s, it was clear the British railway was changing fast. This interior view of the Sighthill freight terminal in Glasgow presents a very different picture to other earlier period shots included in this book, and to the idea of a traverser enabling rail vehicles to be loaded or unloaded more quickly. *British Railways*

BOTTOM RIGHT Plymouth Friary freight concentration depot – another modernised goods station. This picture, taken on 1 September 1966, shows modern lifting equipment assisting in the discharge of heavy packages from rail vans. This development would certainly reduce the time taken to load or unload wagons. To use the modern term, it improved productivity. *British Railways (Western Region)*

LEFT Millerhall marshalling yard is the subject of this panoramic view taken by British Railways Scottish Region. Taken from above the hump, it shows the up sorting sidings with the control tower on the right. Note the brakevan siding to the left and the clearly defined paths. *British Railways*

Bordesley was a major exchange point for traffic between the LMS and GWR. No attempt would be made at Washwood Heath to sort the GWR traffic into any form of station order; all the wagons would be for GWR destinations and that company would shunt them into trains as required. Our coal wagon would become part of a GWR train for the Banbury marshalling yards, where it would be shunted into a local trip working that would take it to its final destination.

However, it was not always so complicated. A small consignment from, say, a Manchester manufacturer to a London merchant could be collected by road vehicle from the consignee and taken to a Manchester goods station, where it would be loaded into a rail vehicle and taken by train direct to one of the London goods stations. There it would either be unloaded and complete the final part of the journey by road, or else it could either be 'tripped' to a local goods yard, to be unloaded before completing its journey by road, or sent by rail to a private siding and unloaded onsite.

Therefore, while our coal wagon was shunted several times during its journey, our Manchester consignment would be shunted when the rail vehicle carrying it became part of the train conveying it to London, where

same organisation, with the Midland and LNWR as part of the LMS. In terms of efficiency it was not something you would have planned from scratch, although it's fascinating for the modeller. However, as rail-borne goods traffic declined, in particular from the mid-1950s onwards, the British railway system began to contract and the traditional method of handling freight traffic would finally cease. Although by then it was an outdated system, traditional shunting was, in my opinion, far more interesting to watch than what can be seen today and certainly far more interesting to reproduce in model form than today's freight traffic.

It would be totally impossible to reproduce the complete British rail transport system. Model railways can at best represent only a part of the journey taken by a consignment from the sender to the receiver, and perhaps model one or more locations where the vehicle carrying the consignment was shunted. To illustrate the various movements of the wagons involved, let's begin with a hypothetical instance

of coal mined at a colliery in Nottinghamshire and sold to a merchant in the Banbury area. The trip engine that brought empty wagons to the colliery and removed the loaded coal traffic would take the wagon conveying the coal to a marshalling yard, possibility Toton, where it would be shunted into a train for Washwood Heath. When it arrived at Washwood Heath, it would be shunted into a train and sent the short distance to the GWR sidings at Bordesley by a local trip working (see Chapter 6 for a full explanation of this term);

RIGHT This picture underlines the 'sameness' of a marshalling yard in the years that followed the end of steam. Note the sidings full of almost identical wagons, the absence of the colourful liveries carried by the private owner wagons and the small number of locomotives. Without doubt it was more efficient, but it was also far less interesting. This view, taken on 30 August 1985, is of the exchange sidings at Ashington, Northumberland and shows a NCB 0-6-0 diesel No 7; to the right, No 56076 is about to depart with a 'merry-go-round' coal train for Blyth Power Station. *Ian S. Carr*

LEFT Overhead conveyors to carry minerals to their loading points have been used for many years – as with this view of Merehead quarry, looking towards the junction of the branch. Note the new overhead loading equipment in this 28 February 1972 picture, to bring the loads to the wagons that had to be shunted into position and removed once the train was ready to depart. *British Railways*

BELOW We previously illustrated a wagon hoist at Leytonstone on page 15; here we show a later example at Dalmarnock Electric Power Station, Glasgow, photographed on 13 February 1964. Coal was sent in block trains from Westfield opencast coalmine to the power station and shunted via use of traversers; although not easy to replicate, this could be reproduced in model form. *British Railways*

that train was broken up and the wagon carrying the consignment moved into the unloading point. In journey times, the Manchester consignment might have taken place overnight while the coal would take several days to complete the journey.

The modeller who has a small branch station with goods facilities will be able to shunt the vehicles that arrive for unloading and to marshal the outwards traffic – whether they be empties from the coal yard or loads from the goods shed and yard – into a train, probably a local trip working. This will take the traffic to the marshalling yard where, depending upon its destination, it will be shunted into trains that will move the traffic forward either to another marshalling yard or direct to its final destination.

Having looked at hypothetical ideas and seen how even a small layout with limited goods facilities could include shunting in its operational activity, let us return to Camden to examine everything on a large scale. In its original wording (which I have tried to retain, except where I felt some modifications would assist the reader's understanding), the *LMS Magazine* describes how wagon capstans were used in the 1930s.

The author states that at Camden the sidings were laid in parallel lines, with a double line of turntables across them, worked by hydraulic capstans. This meant that a wagon could be transferred across the sidings quickly – without the need to shunt other wagons – and placed on the siding according to its destination, which

explains why wagon turntables were retained into the 1960s. Although not mentioned in the article, traversers were used at some stations for lateral movements either inside or outside the shed, near to the entrance for rail vehicles which operated across all tracks over which the wagons passed in or out of the shed. What turntables and traversers could *not* do was to sort a train into station order; the easiest way to accomplish this was to shunt the train from the end of the siding.

Camden was a goods depot with two purpose-built warehouses that could berth approximately 120 wagons, but part of this station was also a very important traffic

BELOW British Railways freightliners were a feature of railway operating for many years. The wagons carrying the container traffic had to be shunted into position for loading or unloading by overhead cranes. This 10 April 1984 picture was taken at Dudley and shows No 40012 shunting wagons for freightliner traffic. *B. J. Robbins*

Margam Marshalling Yard near Port Talbot was opened on 11 April 1960, one of several new yards built during the British Railways era. Note the tall lamps that provided good lighting for the shunters, which was very different from some of the older yards. In the distance we can see a train of wagons being propelled over the hump, while the 16T mineral wagon in the centre of the picture is on the retarder – which worked much more easily and safely than a man running after it, trying to slow it down by use of a handbrake. *British Railways*

operating (marshalling) yard, which received wagons from many other London depots, for despatch (along with those loaded at Camden itself) by mainline trains to the Midlands and the North. This arrangement of a marshalling yard together with a goods station – with loading and unloading facilities for originating and terminating traffic, along with room to warehouse customers' goods – was not uncommon. If there was not a marshalling yard close to the goods station, then the originating traffic would be taken to a yard that was the starting point for long-distance trains and the inwards traffic would arrive at the marshalling yard to be worked to the goods station for unloading.

At one time the yard at Camden was divided into two parts, one for dealing with upside or incoming and the other for downside or outgoing traffic. From approximately midnight until midday, the whole of the yard was devoted to receiving incoming traffic and, from about midday until midnight, to the despatch of outgoing traffic. In the article the author dealt only with incoming traffic, which he described as the reception of trip workings from various depots in the London area: namely Broad Street, Haydon Square, Poplar, Old Ford, Maiden Lane, Victoria Docks, Thames Wharf and St Pancras Junction (traffic from the Midland Division). This traffic was despatched on the down mainline trains, leaving the question of upside traffic for a future article. (In order to show readers where Camden was in relation to other LMS lines, I have included an extract from an LMS map. *See* opposite.)

The author continued by stating that the total number of sidings in Camden Yard was 37, holding approximately 1,100 wagons, of which 640 wagon lengths were given up to the down working (trains departing from Camden). In addition, eight sidings with a capacity of 200 wagons were set apart for the reception of local trip trains, feeding the turntables, engine departure line and accommodation for surplus traffic. He quoted the number of wagons handled and despatched between 6pm and midnight as being between 900 and 1,000, of which about 225 were loaded in the Camden warehouses. The others, with the exception of about 25 from Willesden,

emanated from Broad Street (which despatched about 300) and stations east of Camden. All these had to be remarshalled into trains on arrival at Camden.

The shunting at Camden was performed equally by locomotives and hydraulic capstans. Two engines assisted in the formation of the mainline trains and there were also 37 turntables, manipulated by 11 hydraulic capstans, employed in the down working. The number of staff engaged was two inspectors, two foremen, eight shunters, two capstan foremen, 23 capstan men and one signalman; total 38. Of two reception roads for traffic from the east of London, accommodating in all some 90 wagons, one was principally used for trips from Broad Street, which formed the nucleus of mainline trains. There were 16 of these trips, 12 of which were worked by through mainline engines and formed, with two exceptions, the front portions from Camden.

Traffic for the north from Broad Street was marshalled in reverse order to that leaving Camden by the same train, so as to simplify detaching work en route. Take for instance the 7pm Camden-Manchester, which was marshalled as follows: engine; (1) Broad Street-Manchester; (2) Broad Street-South and Central Wales; (3) Camden-South and Central Wales; (4) Camden-Manchester; brake. It will be observed that the Broad Street portion had Manchester vehicles in front, whereas the Camden-Manchester vehicles were at the rear. This brought the Welsh portions together in the centre of the train, so that when they were

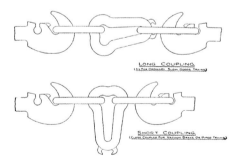

The most common type of coupling was 'three-link', which was used on non-automatic brake goods stock and some locomotives used for shunting or working freight trains. All stock fitted with automatic brakes was generally equipped with screw couplings, with the limited exception of buckeye couplings during the latter part of the steam era. 'Instanter' coupling, like screw coupling, reduced the space between wagon buffers and adjacent wagons, thus ensuring a smoother ride. When vehicles fitted with instanter couplings were in passenger trains, the instruction was to use the screw couplings of the other vehicles and not the instanter couplings, as stipulated in the Railway Companies' 'General Appendix to the Working Time Table'.

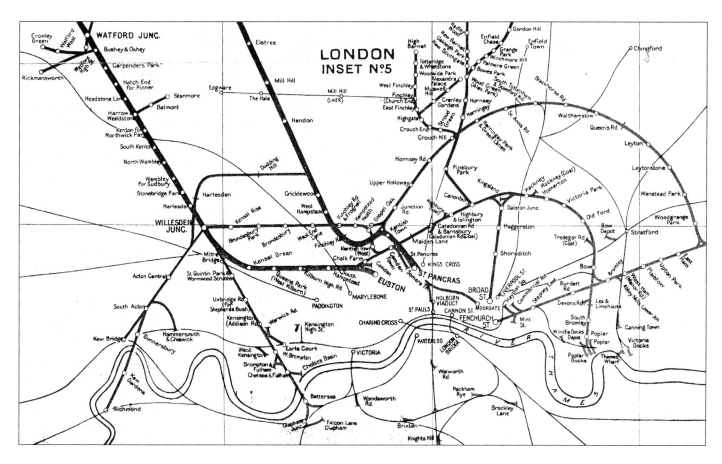

detached at Stafford it was only necessary to unhook portion No 4 and put off Nos 2 and 3 at one shunt. Further, when Nos 4 and 1 were afterwards re-coupled, all the Manchester vehicles were together.

The trips from East London stations also arrived at Camden pre-marshalled to assist in their disposal. Between 12 noon and 6pm, there were 15 such trips with about 250 wagons; between 6pm and 12 midnight there were 10 trips with another 180 wagons. Usually, the rear portion of these trips was put to the turntables over one of the three sidings set apart for the purpose (*see* sketch on p37 for a typical example) or shunted by engine. By this means, the wagons were shunted into their classified road. Great discretion has to be exercised in these movements, owing to the restricted length of the sidings – as a mainline train of 39 or over either fouls the turntables or the exit from the yard, and a train of 49 fouls both. The load of a fully fitted vacuum train is 39 and brake, and that of a loose-coupled train 49 and brake.

There was in practice only one departure line for all mainline trains for the North, and every train arriving from East London stations that required attention prevented any shunting movements along the line by blocking it. To secure satisfactory working in the face of so many structural difficulties, shunting engine movements had to be made to schedule. Thus,

in the case of the 7pm Camden-Manchester referred to above, traffic from stations east of Camden had to be in position by 6.40pm. The Broad Street portion arrived at 6.44pm and attached the Camden-Manchester wagons. The Camden-South and Central Wales portion was then brought along, and as soon as the Broad Street portion had backed up the complete train was despatched. This represents three moves by the capstans, three by the shunting engine and four by the Broad Street portion, totalling 10 moves in about 15 minutes. This applies to a fully-fitted train, but loose-coupled trains are handled with equal promptitude.

Some idea of the amount of work done at Camden traffic yard can be gained from a record taken on a normal day. Between 4.45pm and 11.45pm it shows a total of 47 trip workings; from 6pm to midnight, some 100 moves were made with trip engines, 68 with train engines and 63 with shunting engines – 231 in all. In the vast majority of cases only one movement could be made at a time, and with only a few exceptions each had to be made to schedule if the working was not to be upset.

Much more could be written regarding the working of traffic in Camden Yard, but we can already see what difficulties had to be contended with and how they were overcome.

ABOVE While Camden is in the capital city of London, where there was a large concentration of railways, the principle of a marshalling yard being the focal point where incoming trains were broken up and outgoing trains were assembled remained true throughout the country. It was just the volume of traffic that varied. This map enables readers who may not be familiar with the place names where traffic originated to see where the local London area goods stations were. The map is part of an LMS 1939 edition used by staff. St Pancras Junction was the point where traffic from the Midland Division came onto the Western Division.

It will be recognised how a small upset in the scheduled sequence of movements could disorganise the working of the whole yard. Surely no greater testimony can be given to the excellence of the arrangements and the capability of the staff than the fact that 99 per cent of the traffic received at Camden went forward via its correct service.

My own recollections of express freight trains originating from and terminating at Birmingham goods stations – albeit 20 years later – are similar; prompt working by men and machines, all to a common purpose. The only real difference between my experiences and those of the author of the above article is that diesel-shunting locomotives had by now entered the scene. As we will see in Chapter 6, they were more efficient than the steam locomotives they replaced.

2 Men and equipment

The steam railway was labour intensive. In the previous chapter, the manning level for a shift in the article about Camden Yard should not be taken as a model for all yards. For example, the use of numerous wagon turntables at Camden required 23 men to operate them and a yard would need to be of a certain size to justify an inspector. I suspect that many goods facilities represented on model railways would not justify a foreman; the work would be undertaken by a goods guard and resident shunter instead, who had other duties to perform when not engaged in shunting duties.

To give one personal example, I refer readers to *An Illustrated History of the Ashchurch to Barnt Green Line*, in which I describe a working from Birmingham to Redditch. The train, about 50 wagons in length, arrived after midnight when there were no resident shunters. The work of shunting our wagons into the correct sidings and making up the return train was all in the hands of our guard. It took time to complete, but one man achieved it. Therefore it would probably be correct to say that manning levels were dependent upon the work to be undertaken, but there were always supervisory grades too. At a small station, all staff – probably two porter signalmen and a porter – would be under the control of the stationmaster, while at a major marshalling yard the

yardmaster was in charge, with manning levels similar to those given for Camden or Washwood Heath in *Midland Record No 26*.

The word 'shunting' (see the various definitions in the Introduction) describes both one man pushing a vehicle or doing so with the aid of a pinch bar (also known as a wagon lever), moving vehicles on his own (perhaps in and out of a loading shed or dock) or as part of a collective effort wherein more than one person was engaged. The driver of the shunting engine – with a horse or capstan replacing the locomotive at times – could work only in conjunction with the shunter or guard. However, when moving vehicles as described in the previous chapter, more than one person was usually engaged.

With model railways, it is perfectly possible for one person to control the locomotive and then couple or uncouple the vehicles. However, writing from experience, it is more fun for the driver to drive the locomotive and for another person to couple the vehicles, having already instructed the driver what has to be done or what moves to make.

Signals – hand and verbal
The signals given by the shunter on the full-size railway varied according to conditions. While some were verbal, the majority were hand signals – although, when it became dark, lamps were also used. In the previous chapter I listed the code communicated via the audible signals of bells, gongs, horn or whistles; although the

codes for hand signals will be found on page 111 of *Railway Signalling and Track Plans*, together with a description of how they can be adapted by modellers, I have decided to repeat them here (*see* p30). In *Midland Record No 13* there is an article written by a railwayman who at one time was employed as a shunter. It contains a detailed description of the 'local signals' used by shunters, together with a plan of the sidings. Over the years, similar local signals were used across the British railway system and modellers with yards containing a number of sidings can develop similar signals.

Verbal signals could vary; usually it was a shouted number to identify the siding where the wagon was to be placed, but sometimes codes were used. For example, the sound of numbers seven and 11 are similar and, when shouted, they could be mistaken. This was overcome by using verbal codes; at Washwood Heath, I recall the use of the words 'wax' and 'Nottingham' to replace seven and 11. As with hand signals, there were similar local practices elsewhere which can be adapted for use on model railways.

Shunters and guards

Although the precise term may have varied between companies there were two grades of shunter – head shunter and under shunter – although at many smaller locations there was only one shunter employed. Guards were either 'passenger', 'goods' or 'ballast' guards; my recollection is that, while goods guards used a shunting pole, passenger guards did not. By the early 20th century, safety on railways had become more important and this has continued up into the present day. Rule 12 of the LMS rulebook made it very clear by stressing that shunting poles had to be used when practicable and that the shunter should not throw the link over the drawbar hook until

the buffers had actually touched. This rule contained a number of other clauses stressing safety when coupling vehicles.

One vital piece of equipment was the guard's hand lamp which, when lit, could give either a white, green or red light, the change of colour achieved by a revolving shade inside. In addition, there were three other essential pieces of equipment kept in brakevans which were used in shunting: the brakestick, the shunting pole and sprags, with at least two of these required. Brakesticks were used to apply increased pressure to the vehicle's handbrake lever and sprags were used to prevent wagon wheels from turning when the vehicles were stationary, particularly when left on a gradient.

The responsibility for assembling a goods train in a yard prior to its journey lay with the yard staff, who would use whatever methods were available to them. If it was a hump or gravitation yard, the first vehicles to arrive at the departure end of the siding of a double-ended yard would have their brakes pinned down to act as a 'stop block', thereby ensuring the wagons did not run forward and foul the adjoining lines. Thereafter, wagons would be allowed to roll into the siding and come to a stand against those at the departure end. The final vehicle to be shunted into the siding was the brakevan, but if the shunters started

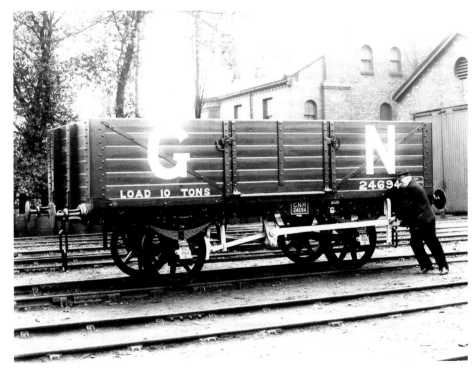

LEFT This undated picture was taken at Feltham and shows a shunter applying handbrakes to a wagon, one of a pair rolling downhill from the hump towards the siding. The difficulty of dealing with wagons with one-sided handbrake levers can be understood fully from this picture. *Ian Allan Library*

RIGHT ABOVE This pre-1923 period picture shows how the use of wagon turntables in conjunction with parallel and right-angle sidings made it possible to transfer wagons from one siding to another by using capstans. Horses were also used to move the wagons in a similar way. *W. O. Steel Collection*

RIGHT BELOW This excellent picture shows a shunter using a brakestick when pinning down the brake lever. The lever was pressed down as far as possible and then a pin attached to a chain was inserted into the holes in the brake lever guard to hold the brake firmly on. *G. Richard Parkes*

LEFT This is a pre-grouping picture (prior to the Great Amalgamation which took place in 1923, when, apart from London Transport, virtually all British railway companies were grouped into the LMS, LNER, GWR or SR) taken on the L&Y, showing a shunter coupling the wagons together by using his shunter's pole – also called, 'catching on' or 'hooking on'. Neither wagon behind him has a brake hand-lever on this side of the wagon.

to make up another train immediately then the first wagons would come up behind the brakevan; the number of wagons in the second train would depend upon how many were in the first and also the length of the siding.

If the shunters were lucky, all the wagons in the first train would be closed together and could be coupled up as they stood but if there were gaps then the train had to be closed up, usually via an engine. With a hump yard this would be done from the departure end, but with a double-ended flat yard closing up could take place at either end. When the train was together with all buffers touching, the brake in the brakevan would be applied. Brakes on the leading wagons would also be on and a shunter would walk along the train, coupling all the wagons together and ensuring that all the handbrakes were off and their levers properly secured in the brake lever guard. Trains were also made up in single-ended sidings and then

drawn out, complete with brakevan, onto the main line or into a loop, either by a shunting engine or the train engine. At this point the train was ready to be handed over to the guard.

The usual arrangement at most marshalling yards was to assemble the train in a siding to await the arrival of the guard and the train engine. The interval between the train being ready and the arrival of the engine and guard would depend upon local circumstances. If it was a weekend and the train was being assembled on a Saturday night, it might be Monday afternoon before it departed. The locomotive and enginemen came from the motive power department, while the goods guard belonged to the traffic department; at some locations, the guards booked on for duty at the same place as the enginemen. The enginemen and their locomotive did not require very much time after backing onto the train before they were ready to

depart, as coupling the engine to the wagons and setting the headlamps was all that had to be done.

The guard, who generally arrived before the train engine, began by checking with the yard staff, shunters, inspector or whoever else was in charge to confirm he was taking over the train. Then he would walk along the train to check all was in order – brakes secure, wagon and van doors properly closed, tarpaulin sheets tied and any overhanging loads correctly marshalled – and to 'note the load', recording the classification and number of vehicles to ensure the train did not exceed the loading limit for its class of locomotive. This information would be given to the driver. He would probably walk along one side to the brakevan, leave his 'traps' (belongings) in the van, maybe light the fire and check that the side and tail lamps were ready for use. Then, with his shunting pole, he would walk along the other side of the train towards the engine, although there were also times when brakevans were prepared by a shunter in order to ensure a speedy departure.

By the time he reached the engine it would be close to departure time. All he had to do was tell the driver what the load was – i.e. how many wagons he was hauling, their weight and the length of the train – plus any other instructions, before returning to his van. Depending upon circumstances, the train

ABOVE The use of shunter's trucks was most common on the GWR, and later the Western Region of British Railways. However, as we can see from this pre-grouping picture of Maryport & Carlisle Railway 0-4-0T No 2, other companies also used them.

ABOVE The uniform style for guards and shunters was similar across all British railway companies. This picture shows a young Midland Railway shunter with his 'pole' or 'badge of office', which would also have been held by men from other railway companies in a similar manner.
D. F. Tee

ABOVE Here we see a shunter holding a sprag; another sprag is between the spokes of the wagon wheel to prevent the vehicle from moving.
Kidderminster Railway Museum

may have started before he reached the brakevan and so the guard would jump onto his brakevan while it was on the move, exchanging hand signals with the fireman to let the enginemen know the train was complete. But otherwise he would return to his brakevan and wait for the train to start, exchanging hand signals with the fireman as soon as the train began to move.

The signal to start the train could be given by the guard, but if he had returned to his brakevan a shunter, or the man in charge of the sidings, would give the signal. This was in accordance with Rule 108 of the *Railway Company Rule Book* (the big four companies' rules being virtually identical) which states, 'during shunting operations Drivers must work only to the signals given by the Guard, Shunter or other person in charge and must not move his train until he has received such a signal although the fixed signal may have been lowered.'

Throughout the UK there were numerous unusual working arrangements. See (on pp36-7) the example from Desford colliery, where the

LEFT This unusual view of a GWR shunter's truck at Lydney Town was photographed on 22 July 1972, almost four years after the end of steam on British Railways. It shows the footboard and handrails that were used by shunters. Quite what modern Health and Safety would say about the working practices of the day is another matter!

were necessary but nor could the driver have seen any, owing to the curve in the siding – which is why the procedure was initiated.

Control of points

The control of points in goods and marshalling yards varied. Some were worked from a signalbox or ground frame, but an adjacent hand lever controlled the majority of points. Some signalboxes – generally at the entrance to or the exit from the yards – would be block posts but most would not, merely controlling the pointwork within the yard. Signalboxes within the yard itself would only be found at the larger goods sidings, but one feature we will encounter in Chapter 4 can also be modelled: the lever frame or 'stage', often found at a location where there was a signalbox controlling the running lines but where the entrance or exit to the goods yard was beyond the distance allowed to work points by rodding, thus making other arrangements necessary. At these locations, railway companies installed a lever frame that was bolted (i.e. locked) by the signalbox. When a train was to go into or come out of the sidings, the train's guard or shunter asked the signalman to release the bolt; this enabled the points and signals (if any) to be controlled from the stage and the train would

sidings layout required departing trains destined for Coalville to adopt a special way of working. The engine was coupled to the train at the colliery end of the sidings (there was a falling gradient towards the main line) with the brakevan at the mainline end of the train. Just prior to departure, the guard would apply the brake in his van and a couple of wagon brakes, just enough to hold the train. (The engine stood with the brakes off.) When the outlet signal came off, the guard released the wagon brakes and the train slowly rolled out of the sidings into a neck before stopping, then reversing and proceeding towards Coalville. The initial movement of the train indicated to the driver that the outlet signal was off. No hand signals

RIGHT This is another view of an LMS petrol-driven shunting tractor (see previous example in Chapter 1). This particular picture was taken to show how they could cross over sidings.

ABOVE/RIGHT On the right we show the 'slow down' hand signal; above we see the signal being given by a guard. The extract from the rulebook gives a piece of very essential information about communications between drivers and other railwaymen. The signals are self-explanatory. If modellers use their fingers to replicate them, it is quite easy for one acting as a shunter or guard to signal to the modeller controlling the locomotive. There is therefore no need for modern electrical devices that are far removed from the reality of the era we are trying to reproduce.

Rule 51

Rule 51

Danger or stop signal.

51. In the absence of flags—
(a) Both arms raised above the head denotes Danger or stop:—
(NOTE.—When riding on or in a vehicle either arm moved up and down denotes stop.)

Move away from hand signal.

(d) Either arm moved in a circular manner away from the body denotes move away from hand signal, thus:—

Caution or slow down signal.

(b) Either arm held in a horizontal position and the hand moved up and down denotes Caution or slow down, thus:—

Move towards handsignal.

(e) Either arm moved across and towards the body at shoulder level denotes move towards hand signal, thus:—

All Right signal.

(c) Either arm held above the head denotes All Right, thus:—

Create vacuum.

(f) Arm moved vertically up and down above shoulder level denotes create vacuum, thus:—

set back into the sidings, so that shunting could commence. Once in the sidings, the levers would be restored and the frame bolted normally so that running on the main line could recommence. The same arrangement applied when the train was to depart.

Although it is modern modelling practice to control all points by electric motors, hand-worked points have been installed in the coal yard on the Dewsbury layout on display at the HMRS Museum and Study Centre. The idea was to show how the shunter had to move between the points in order to reverse them, but beneath the baseboard a simple micro-switch ensures the electricity supply is maintained. Running alongside wagons to apply the brakes in poorly lit yards, jumping over rails and other obstructions were all rather hazardous, which is why many men were killed or injured each year undertaking this work.

Summary – signals: fixed and hand, flags and lamps

Although I have previously mentioned various forms of signals, I have summarised the hand signals using flags and lamps here. For modellers, I would say that if there are two operators – one driving the engine and the other acting as shunter – then it is far better if conversation is kept to a minimum and hand signals are used. By using the hand or finger, the beckoning 'come towards' signal

and the circular 'move away' signal are simple to perform. Moving the fingers up and down will represent 'slow down' and the unmoving palm of the hand shows the 'stop' signal, with a slight wave of the hand giving the 'right away' signal to the driver. Although I have seen this form of hand signal used on model railways, I have never seen hand lamps used to display signs – the most obvious of which would be a green light to indicate 'right away' to the driver.

Couplings – prototype and as used by modellers

My modelling experience with couplings has only been on a 4mm or 7mm scale. Having changed to the latter 30 years ago, I recognise there have been many changes (in particular on the smaller scales) during this period. Couplings on models have always been a problem and we have already mentioned the three types used on the prototype: link, screw and, to a very limited extent, automatic couplings. I will concentrate upon couplings used by modellers. Without doubt, the smaller the scale the more difficult it becomes as 'the hand of God' is obliged to use its miniature coupling stick. However, a story of an encounter when this book was being written may help to set the scene.

I was at the HMRS Museum and Study Centre during one of their open days. I had emerged from below the Dewsbury Goods Station layout baseboards when a youth of about 13 spoke to me. He had been looking intently at the Plemsworth layout, which is close to Dewsbury. 'Is this 00?' was his opening remark. 'Yes and no,' was my reply, 'the bodies of the locomotives and stock are to 4mm scale but the gauge of the track on this layout is 18.83mm, whereas 00 is 16.5mm.'

'I like the way the buffers touch each other,' he said.

'That is because they can use scale couplings, not auto couplings, which are required if 00 trains are to run round sharp curves.'

There was a long pause before his verdict. 'I prefer the buffers to touch each other.' The opportunity to discuss the pros and cons of the two systems was lost when his grandfather arrived and said it was time to move to the next exhibit. What this young man had recognised is that on the smaller scales – 4mm and below – it is common practice to use non-prototypical items to ensure good running, but when this happens it is more difficult to achieve realism in miniature. Much has been written about couplings in the model press, and suffice it to say that coupling and uncoupling on the smaller scales is not easy. One solution is to use magnets at track level to disengage the couplings, but this (and other similar fixed devices) reduces the flexibility obtained by the man with a shunting stick.

BELOW This picture was probably taken to show how a man should *not* pin down wagon brakes. The shunter is using the end of his coupling pole, which was forbidden; the correct method was to use a purpose-made brakestick (see page 27). *Ian Allan Library*

RIGHT The No 1 label was for coal traffic, in this case a consignment from Haunchwood colliery to Studley, dated 6 February 1960 and consigned to the Alcester Co-Op on the account of the CWS Manchester. The route was via Washwood Heath marshalling yard; the wagon was a BR 16T vehicle; the weight of the consignment of washed nuts was 11 tons 18 cwt. A loaded 16 ton wagon was rated as equal to 1⅓ 13T mineral wagons, an important factor to be taken into account when shunting a train made up of both 13T and 16T. If the loading for a particular class of engine was equal to 48 wagons and the train included six '16-tonners', then the train would be overloaded if there were more than 46 mineral wagons coupled to the engine. This all had to be worked out on the spot in all weather conditions without the aid of calculators!

FAR RIGHT ABOVE The wagon label provided the necessary information about the load and where it was going, in this case concentrated fertilizer sent from Haverton Hill to Studley and Astwood bank, routed via marshalling yards at Dringhouses and Washwood Heath. The wagon number was B773518 and it was consigned to Worcestershire Farmers. There were three categories of traffic displayed on the wagon labels: '1' was coal; '2' was other minerals; '3' was goods traffic. This information was required by the shunters and guards when making up a train to ensure it was not overloaded for the class of engine that was to pull it.

RIGHT The following appears in the *LMS Loading of Passenger and Freight Trains Loading Book*, dated 1 October 1945: 'Passenger engines working Freight Trains will take one-tenth less load than freight engines of similar classification.' The LMS used a system of power classification that was later adopted by British Railways, although prior to nationalisation all the railway companies had similar methods of classifying train loading. There were a maximum number of vehicles in length that could be conveyed by any class of train over a given stretch of line and also a maximum load for the various classes of locomotives. To further complicate matters, wagons were classified as 'mineral', 'goods' or 'empties', and when marshalling trains these calculations had to be taken into account by shunters and guards. To illustrate this, I have included part of pp7-8 from the railway company instructions (*Right*).

LEFT The use of lines that ran at right angles to sidings enabled goods vehicles to be shunted between sidings in the open yard, within a large goods shed or between the shed and the yard. Although horses were used, the most common method was by capstan – as in these two pictures. (*Above*) This view was taken in the open yard and shows how easy it was to transfer the covered goods van from one siding to another via two wagon turntables and the transverse connecting road. Note the capstan man with his foot on the stop to prevent movement of the wagon turntable once the move has been completed. The other capstan man is controlling the movement of the wagon turntable, so that it will stop with the rails aligned to the siding where the van is to be placed. (*Below*) This wagon turntable, seen at Wolverhampton Mill Street goods station in January 1932, is set for the transverse road. As the picture shows, it was not necessary for the sidings to be at right angles; the controlling factor was the wheelbase of the goods wagon being shunted and anything over about ten feet was too long. *NRM DY 17187*

4. CALCULATIONS OF EQUIVALENT LOADINGS

In calculating the loading of freight trains :—

3½ wagons of goods
or
5 empty wagons
} equal 2 wagons of mineral.

Wagons bearing labels endorsed "1" or "2" must be counted as "mineral."

Wagons bearing labels endorsed "3" must be counted as "Goods."

The loading of fitted freight trains, express freight trains and through freight trains, is published in "Wagons of goods" and when traffic of the weight of mineral is conveyed by these freight trains, two such wagons must be reckoned as 3½ wagons of goods.

The loading of mineral trains is published in "Wagons of mineral" and the unit of loading for mineral trains is a loaded 13-ton wagon, wagons of less capacity being counted as 13-ton wagons.

The method of calculating empty wagons as five equal to two wagons of mineral to be applied to all ordinary types of empty wagons of less carrying capacity than 15-tons. Empty wagons of exceptional length to be counted as two empties.

LOADING OF FREIGHT TRAINS (continued)

5. MATCH WAGONS

For the purpose of calculating the load of a train, match wagons for long loads should be counted as empty wagons, but such wagons should be entered on the Guard's Journal as loaded wagons.

6. CALCULATION OF EQUIVALENTS FOR SPECIAL TYPES OF WAGONS

The undermentioned types of wagons and other vehicles including engines (not in steam) will be calculated as follows :—

Description of wagons, etc.	Contents	No. of wagons, etc.	Equal to No. of 13-ton wagons of mineral
14 to 21-ton	Goods	3	4
14 to 21-ton	Mineral	2	3
15 to 24-ton	Empty	3	2
22 to 24-ton	Goods	2	3
22 to 24-ton	Mineral		2
25 to 40-ton	Goods	1	3
25 to 40-ton	Empty	2	3
25 to 40-ton	Mineral	2	7
10 and 12-ton tank	Loaded	4	5
14 and 15-ton tank	Loaded	2	3
10, 12, 14 and 15-ton tank	Empty	3	1
20-ton tank	Loaded	2	4
20-ton tank	Empty	3	2
35-ton tank	Loaded	2	7
35-ton tank	Empty	2	3
40-ton tank	Loaded	2	7
40-ton tank	Empty	2	3
U.S.A. Bogie Tank	Loaded	1	3
U.S.A. Bogie Tank	Empty	1	1
50-ton Warflat or Warwell	Empty	1	3
50-ton Warflat or Warwell	Loaded	1	4
Bogie refrigerator vans-lettered "US Transportation Corps"	Loaded	1	2
Bogie refrigerator vans-lettered "US Transportation Corps"	Empty	2	3
6-wheeled rail vehicles conveying road rail tanks		1	2
Bogie Passr. vehicles, not exceeding 30-tons	Empty	2	3
Bogie Passr. vehicles, exceeding 30 tons	Empty	1	2
Motor vans (6 or 8 wheeled)	Loaded	1	1
Rail wagons	Loaded with rails	1	1
Sludge tenders	Loaded	1	3
Sludge tenders	Empty	2	3
Small tank engines, or engine tenders		1	2
Small types of engines with tenders		1	4
Large types of engines with tenders		1	6

ABOVE During the steam era there was a lot of paperwork required, as this picture shows. The record of exchange of wagons and sheets (wagon tarpaulins) at junctions between two companies was undertaken by the railway clearing house or by railway company staff. The object was to maintain the book stock of common user wagons, demurrage (transit) for non-common user wagons and journey payment for common user wagons. Each of the big four had a book stock of common user wagons, with the number of each type balanced on a weekly basis. The picture shows an LMS railwayman engaged in what was commonly known as number taking.

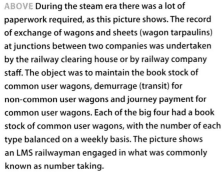

LEFT If they were carrying this label then the wagons were not going anywhere; they were stopped for repairs.

ABOVE Dating from 1941, this 'Shunt With Great Care' label was for a wagon from Stevenston to Thrumster via High Shields, Perth and Dunkeld. There is no information about what the load was, but the outside goods sheds suggest explosive or flammable material.

LEFT This picture shows a goods guard and shunter carrying their shunting poles, plus either an inspector or stationmaster. In terms of responsibility, the guard was in charge of the train, the inspector of the sidings; if he were a stationmaster, then he would be responsible for the sidings only if they were part of his station.

RIGHT ABOVE Photographed at Mottram Yard, which is near to Manchester on the Woodhead line, the foreman announces a 'cut' over the tannoy – a railway term for one or more wagons that have been uncoupled during shunting. The foreman is telling his shunters to 'set the road' for the siding that the cut is to run into, as the train rolls off the reception line down the bank towards the sorting sidings. *G. Richard Parkes*

RIGHT BELOW The classic 'right away' signal from the guard to driver is shown here. As soon as the signal was acknowledged the guard would return to his brakevan, which could have been moving. Goods guards were agile enough to jump onto a moving van, although the need to exchange hand signals with the fireman ensured the driver knew the guard was safely on board before they went very far from the starting point.

LEFT Wagon turntables are rarely featured on model railways, which is a pity as they were an important part of goods traffic working. This close-up view has been included to show how the wooden planks were set each side of the rails, with two catches opposite each other to lock the table into position. In model form they can be worked by an electric motor, but personal experience suggests a simple worm and wheel hand-driven arrangement is ideal. *Michael Andress*

BELOW There were locations where access to goods yards and private sidings was controlled by a lever frame that had to be unlocked before the points could be changed and the engine/train entered. Then shunting could begin and the same procedure followed when it was time to depart. This usually applied when the points controlling the connection with the siding were too far away from the signalbox to be worked manually, whereupon the shunter or guard would contact the signalman to get him to unlock the ground frame. (There is a section dealing with this subject in *Railway Signalling and Track Plans*.) The diagram is based upon the track layout at Dunlop & Co's private sidings near Castle Bromwich, Birmingham, but similar arrangements could be found elsewhere throughout the country. This particular example of a private siding connection provides considerable modelling potential.

Diagram to show stage bolt locked by signalbox, based upon Dunlop & Co private sidings

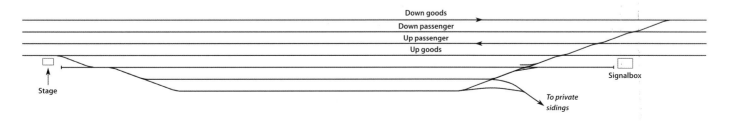

Desford Colliery sidings from December 14 December, 1970

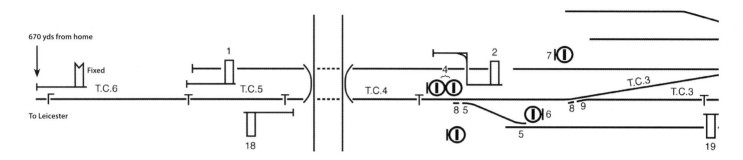

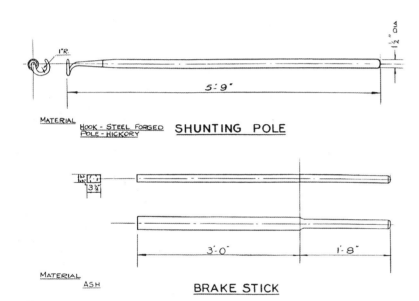

MATERIAL HOOK - STEEL FORGED POLE - HICKORY

SHUNTING POLE

MATERIAL ASH

BRAKE STICK

Drawing by Denis G. Monk, C. Eng., M.I. Mech. E.

ABOVE In order to get to the head of the train, the light engine normally ran along the empty wagon line and set back onto the train at the colliery end of the sidings. On occasion, if there was an empty road in the loaded wagon sidings, the engine would sometimes run up it to the colliery end. If an engine and brake came from Coalville to work a train back, the brakevan would be trailing from Coalville so that, on arrival, it could be set back into the loaded wagon sidings and straight onto the loaded train. The engine then made its way to the colliery end of the loaded wagon sidings.

Desford colliery was strange because, when it opened *c*1904, the sidings, mainline connections and signalling were laid out for loads to depart towards and empties to return from the direction of Leicester. In the 1950s, track and signalling alterations were made to permit empty wagon trains from the east to run straight into the empties sidings. Then, possibly in the 1960s, the traffic flow changed round completely, with loads departing towards and empties returning from the direction of Coalville. However, the sidings were the wrong way around to do that and some minor modifications had to be made to the layout, with special shunting arrangements put in place.

Typical modeller's shunting pole

Most modellers tend to use a shunting pole with the hook as an extension (see sketch), but it is much easier if you use one of the same shape as the full-sized version. My method of coupling stock is to use this type of pole for loose couplings and some screw couplings, but generally I find long straight tweezers better for coupling coaching stock if vacuum and steam-heat pipes, and maybe corridor connections, are to be avoided.

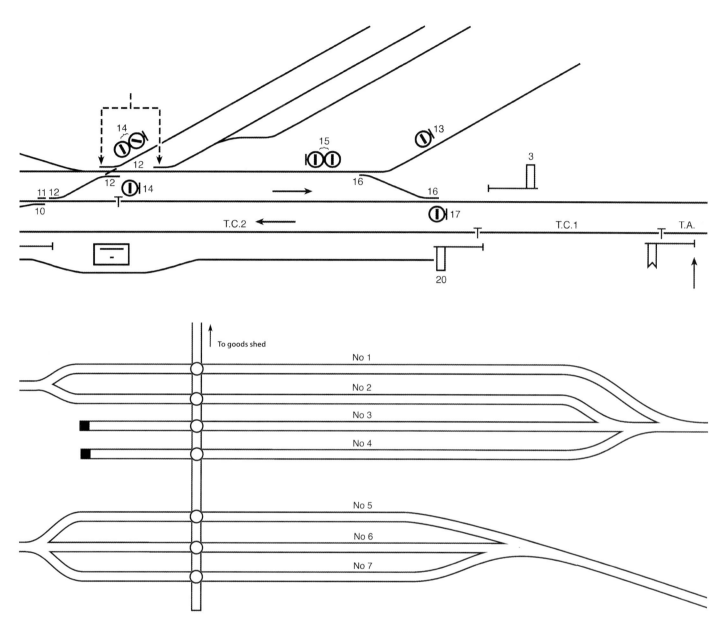

ABOVE As can be gleaned from this simple sketch, the arrangement of wagon turntables varied. It shows two groups of sidings – Nos 1-4 and 5-7 – with turntables that enabled wagons to be transferred between any of the sidings via the traverse road. Although a locomotive could do this, using capstans and ropes to haul the wagons along the sidings and the turntables to transfer the wagons between sidings was less disruptive. This was particularly true in an open yard when loading or unloading wagons might also be taking place.

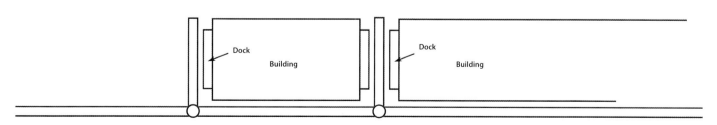

ABOVE Of particular interest to modellers may be the arrangement shown, whereby a wagon could be moved to an unloading dock without the space required for points and sidings. This arrangement offers considerable potential for modellers whose space is restricted. As can also be seen in *Railways of England*, if this arrangement with a large building is used then one dock can be for loading or unloading goods while the other might contain coal for the boilers, etc.

3 Shunting and marshalling passenger trains and stock

The suggestion that coaches were shunted usually elicits a look of disbelief from the listener, who no doubt is visualising coaches being shunted over a hump. But, as we will see, coaches were most definitely shunted by gravity. The opportunities to use flat shunting carriages in model railways based on the steam era are considerable, as we will also see in this chapter. But first we must define carriage stock.

To put it in simple terms: from the late Victorian period, vehicles designed to run in passenger trains had to have automatic brakes – either vacuum or Westinghouse, or through pipes to allow the vehicle to be coupled to automatic braked stock. There were requirements regarding the wheelbase that varied over the years, and readers will find further information on this in *Passenger Train Operation for the Railway Modeller*. The stock used in passenger trains was described as either Non-Passenger Carrying Coaching Stock (NPCS) or Passenger Carrying Coaching Stock, further complicated by the fact that

passenger brake vans – which did not carry passengers – were usually to be found in the railway company's passenger-coaching stock diagram book.

Railway companies usually kept four reference books that contained dimensioned diagrams for all the stock owned by them: passenger carrying, non-passenger carrying, freight stock and specially designed freight stock vehicles. While this has little to do with shunting, it is important to have an understanding of the various types of vehicles and of where NPCS could be marshalled in passenger trains. There were also a number

of rules that applied to shunting carriages, as already mentioned in Chapter 1.

The composition of trains was carefully regulated and shown in the relevant company documents; extracts from some LMS examples appear on page 51. This information was circulated each time there was a change of working time table, which was usually two or three times a year. It showed the order in which the vehicles were assembled in the train, the seating capacity, the destination of each vehicle, the previous working of the stock and the weight of each train. The actual circuit working of all coaches was shown in other

LEFT When not in use, carriages were usually held in sidings at or close to passenger stations, or at carriage sheds where it was usual practice to clean the vehicles on a regular basis. One feature of carriage sheds was the raised platform for the cleaners to stand on when working with the long-handled brushes that were used to clean the windows and sides. Because carriages were usually kept in sets, shunting them at the sheds was fairly simple. This picture was taken at Cricklewood on 17 March 1921.

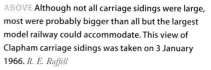
ABOVE Although not all carriage sidings were large, most were probably bigger than all but the largest model railway could accommodate. This view of Clapham carriage sidings was taken on 3 January 1966. *R. E. Ruffell*

documents; examples are shown on page 51 and it should be stressed that, although they are examples of LMS practice, the other major British railway companies (and later British Railways) also used similar documents. The principle governing the composition of trains was based upon train ticket collectors' loading returns, guards' journals, stationmasters' reports and overall company policy. The traffic departments of the railways used these sources to determine the composition of trains, e.g. if a train normally carried 100 passengers per trip there was no need for more than three coaches; if a train used to carry 500 but was now carrying only 200, the number of coaches could be reduced.

As with goods trains, there were authorised maximum loads for passenger trains over given lines that varied according to the class of locomotive and the gradient. On some LMS trains there was a requirement that the first-class, sleeping and dining-car accommodation should be, as far as possible, in the centre of the train; dining-car accommodation also had to be adjacent to the seating accommodation of the same class, but with other companies first class was usually at the 'buffers end' of the platform serving the principal station. (The first-class carriages would be at the end of the train, close to the

exit. For example, a train to Euston would have the first-class coaches marshalled behind the engine, which meant less distance for the first-class passenger to walk to the taxi rank.) There were also restrictions regarding the marshalling of four-wheeled stock, for example where horseboxes, milk or parcels vans should be in the train.

Detailed information about the composition of passenger trains may be found in *Passenger Train Operation for the Railway Modeller*; in this part of the series, I have tried to concentrate upon factors surrounding marshalling and composition of the trains. Many trains used on long-distance services included non-lavatory stock; when this occurred, it was desirable to include a corridor or non-corridor lavatory coach in the train. The practice was to try to place a brake vehicle at the front of express

trains with the brake compartment next to the engine, and to provide sufficient first-class and brakevan accommodation with trains formed of open – or, as the LMS called it, 'vestibule' – stock.

Another feature found on the steam railway was through-carriages. This service enabled a passenger to enter a carriage at station A in order to travel to station X, even if the train was not going to X. When it stopped at station B, the coach would be removed from the first train and added to another train that was going to station X. A station pilot usually undertook this work, although in some circumstances a train engine would make the necessary shunting moves. Rarely seen on model railways, it was normal practice at many junction stations.

When marshalling local passenger trains, which could be a formation used for short distance residential travel, various combinations could be used. It could be a formation used for short-distance residential travel, branch line trains and passenger trains that acted as feeders for express trains. These combinations would vary depending upon the time of day and the precise route. The sets could be made up using corridor, lavatory or

LEFT This shows part of the much smaller sidings at Truro when photographed on 1 November 1969. *M. H. C. Baker*

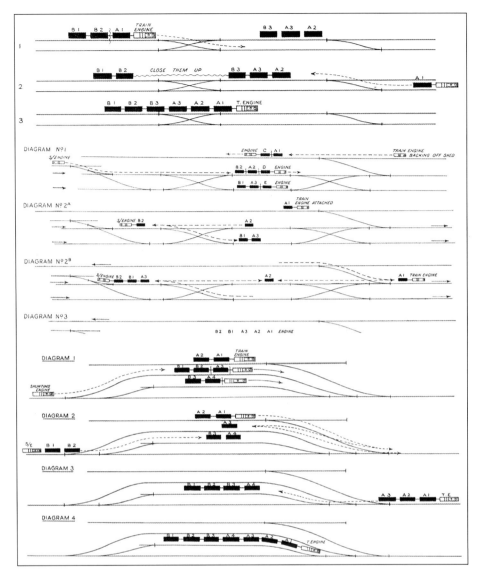

These 11 diagrams have been reproduced from a training manual used by the LMS at their school for members of staff. I have retained the original text and, although not always easy to understand, it gives examples of how trains can be divided or combined. In each case the key is the scissors crossing. I suggest that readers look at the sequence of moves first, then read the accompanying text. If modellers wish to incorporate combining or dividing passenger trains on their layouts, then they must design the track to accommodate the moves they wish to make. (NB: 'T. Engine' is train engine; the station pilot is always referred to as 'Shunting Engine' or 'S/Engine'.)

[*Top Left*] Diagram [1-3] showing the method of combining two trains, each with portions for two destinations, by using a scissors crossing. The first train is run beyond the scissors crossing and the engine detached, the second train arriving with a portion to be attached in front of the first train, with the engine of the second train working the combined train forward. The engine of the second train travels via the scissors crossing and backs on to the first train, afterwards propelling vehicles to those left standing towards the rear of the platform. The combined train is now ready to leave with vehicles for each destination properly marshalled.

[*Centre Left*] Diagram [*No. 1/2a/2b/3*] showing the movements made in combining vehicles of three trains, a fresh engine being provided to take the train forward. In each case the trains arriving convey local portions, lettered 'C''D' and 'E' respectively. After their departure the remaining vehicles from each of the trains are combined in marshalling order, facilitated by the use of a scissors crossing.

[*Bottom Left*] Diagram [*1-4*] illustrating where the vehicles from three trains have to be combined without the use of a scissors crossing, the engine of one of the trains working the combined train forward.

Readers will find a number of passenger station track plans in *Passenger Train Operation for the Railway Modeller*; in this book I have only included examples where shunting took place.

Some shunting movements required vehicles to be coupled to both ends of the locomotive. This picture of 0-6-0T No 30072 shunting at Guildford in October 1966 illustrates the arrangement. *Peter Tatlow*

Photographed on 23 April 1975, a Class 08 propels a train of empty stock into the platform at Penzance to form the 14.40 express passenger train to Paddington. *Brian Morrison*

non-lavatory coaches and coupled into sets of two, three or more vehicles according to the general requirements of the district. The daily working of these vehicles would be set out in the carriage working diagrams showing when the units were coupled to other units to form longer trains, or reduced in size when the level of traffic declined.

This method of train working was very different from that practised today. The principle in use was to provide for the laid-down service efficiently, with the minimum amount of stock to achieve the maximum use. Other factors that played a part in train formation were the reduction of empty carriage working and the time required by the carriage and wagon department for regular cleaning and overhaul, so that, although the amount of shunting was minimal when compared with goods stock, it did take place at carriage sidings, carriage washing plants and many stations where the composition of trains was altered by the addition or removal of

carriages during the course of the day. Train formations were changed to meet traffic needs, but trains comprising only a few carriages would always include at least one with a guard's compartment, even if it was a single-coach train.

Excursion trains were a major feature during most of the steam era and the make-up of their sets of carriages varied. Some trains consisted of carriages that came from other trains that would not be running when the excursion train was operating, a process described as 'rediagramming local train circuits'. Long-distance trains made up of corridor or open stock often included dining cars that helped to maximise the use of catering facilities owned by the company. The work of making up most of these trains was usually undertaken in carriage sidings, while some stock for other trains – which consisted of almost time-expired coaches that may have been used only a few times per year – were kept at suitable sidings when not required.

The use of gravity to shunt carriages is not easy to achieve on model railways, although I have seen it in action on the 4mm-scale Wellington layout; watching the carriages come down a gradient and stop at a platform was fascinating. Before we consider how this can be achieved on a model railway, we must examine the methods used on the prototype.

There were various ways whereby coaches were moved to a platform. They could be drawn into a dead-end platform line by an engine working tender-first that would be used as a train engine for a subsequent train, or by

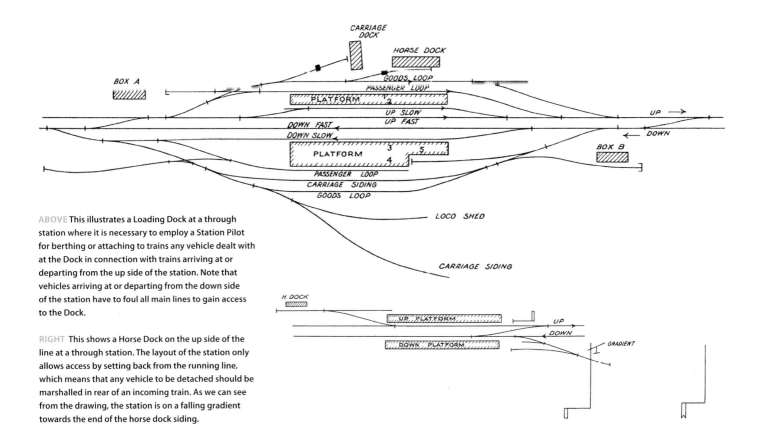

ABOVE This illustrates a Loading Dock at a through station where it is necessary to employ a Station Pilot for berthing or attaching to trains any vehicle dealt with at the Dock in connection with trains arriving at or departing from the up side of the station. Note that vehicles arriving at or departing from the down side of the station have to foul all main lines to gain access to the Dock.

RIGHT This shows a Horse Dock on the up side of the line at a through station. The layout of the station only allows access by setting back from the running line, which means that any vehicle to be detached should be marshalled in rear of an incoming train. As we can see from the drawing, the station is on a falling gradient towards the end of the horse dock siding.

a shunting engine that would be available for banking if such a move were authorised. But this method meant the shunting engine was not available until after the passenger train had departed, unless there was an independent turn out road leading from the stop blocks that permitted the release of the shunting engine. Another way was to propel the coaches into the station by the engine that worked the train forward, or for the coaches to be propelled into the platform by a shunting engine.

Gravitating coaches into a station saved a subsequent move in the disposal of the engine, with the platform and main lines consequently cleared more quickly for other station movements. By diagramming an engine to work in tender-first when drawing the empty coaches into a dead-end line, the engine quickly became available for working a subsequent loaded train and the move often involved the minimum line occupation. This way of working was in force at many of the larger terminal stations and was of particular value where groups of excursion trains were leaving the station in close sequence.

If the train was propelled into the station by the engine that was subsequently to work the loaded train forward, line occupation was saved, platform road occupation may have been curtailed and the greatest use made of the platform itself by virtually its full length being available for the coaches. Preheating may also have been facilitated by this method. Occasionally propelling by a shunting engine instead of the train engine may have been desirable when the maximum empty coach siding accommodation was required and a departure platform was available for a period in advance of the actual train departure. Thus the platform road became temporarily a carriage siding.

Such facilities existed at certain platforms at some terminal stations. I'm aware from personal experience that this applied at Birmingham (New Street) station, which was both a terminal and a through station. Facilities for drawing complete but empty

LEFT As we have seen, carriage sidings at major centres were large. This is the view from the roof of the new carriage shed at Willesden, 23 February 1953. *British Railways*

RIGHT Cannock carriage sidings, 7 May 1963. Cannock is near Wolverhampton and many miles from Cricklewood, but the methods used at Cricklewood some 42 years earlier were continued in many carriage sidings. The note on the reverse of the print states that some 50 coaches were cleaned by hand daily at Cannock. Here, one of the Western Region 'chocolate and cream' coaches is dealt with. *Ian Allan Library*

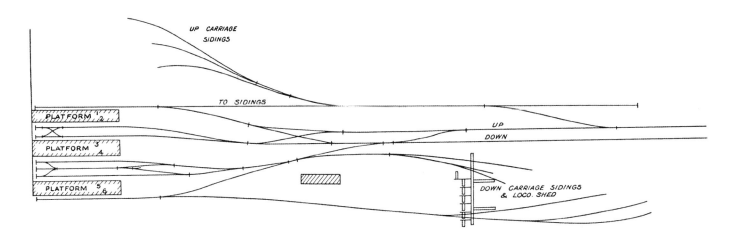

ABOVE This diagram shows various phases of operation at a terminal station where the Carriage Sidings are situated in rear of the arrival platform. In this case, the train engine propelling coaches from platforms 4, 5 and 6 to the Down Carriage Sidings can dispose of arriving trains. Trains arriving at platforms 1, 2 and 3 can be disposed of by a Station Pilot to the Up Carriage Sidings. From platform roads 4 and 5 the train engine can be released on arrival through the turnout road. From platform roads 2 and 3 the engine can be released through the unoccupied platform road. From platform roads 1 and 6 the train would have to be drawn from the platform by a Station Pilot in order to release the train engine. The empty stock for starting trains can be berthed by train engines propelling from both the Up and Down Carriage Sidings either direct or by means of a double shunting movement.

RIGHT Long-distance parcels trains connected with traffic from over a wide area. Even if your layout represents a branch line in a country district, there could be a reason why parcel traffic was part of your operational sequence. This route diagram shows the feeding and distributing train routes that connected with the 8.55pm parcels train from Euston to Carlisle. Similar diagrams would apply to all the main lines of the big four British railway companies.

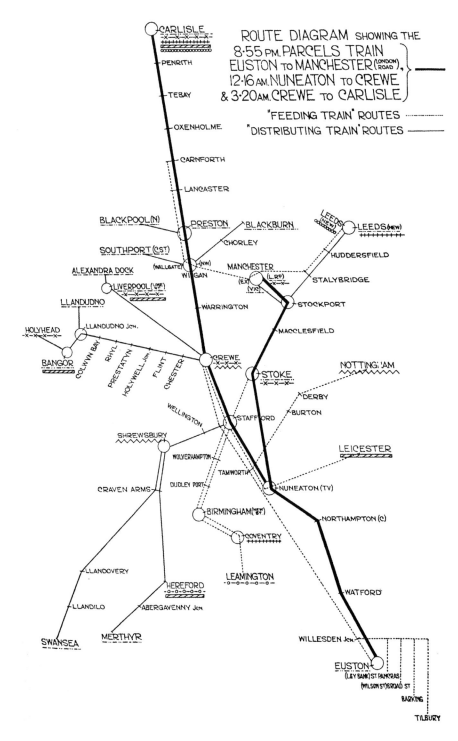

ABOVE This undated view of Willesden carriage sidings provides a good idea of the expanse covered by major carriage installations, although at stations it was mostly common practice to have two smaller carriage sidings, one each side of the station – the distance from station to shed varying from quite close by to several miles. This made the movement of stock less difficult and provides modellers with a reason for a smaller installation. The unidentified Stanier 4-6-0 locomotive has either brought a train of empty stock to the sidings or is to take one away. *Ian Allan Library*

ABOVE TOP LEFT This picture of the new carriage-washing plant at Clapham was taken on 20 January 1949. Modernisation of the plants was necessary and the Southern Railway probably ordered this model before nationalisation. *British Railways (Southern Region)*

ABOVE TOP RIGHT Not all carriage-washing plants were large; this rather small plant was photographed at Bournemouth West on 4 September 1965. *A. J. Wheeler*

CENTRE LEFT A few years before this picture was taken on 24 February 1968, a steam locomotive – possibly a shunting engine, a station pilot or the train engine – would have been at the head of this train of empty carriages. Hauled by 'Peak' class 45 No D24, the train is approaching Bristol Temple Meads and will form the 15.30 express passenger train to York. *P. J. Fowler*

CENTRE RIGHT Eleven years after the end of steam traction on British Railways, the old methods of working trains continued. Here we see a Class 03 shunter No 03073 hauling a train of empty coaching stock that formed the 08.05 express from King's Cross to Hull. This picture was taken at Hull Paragon station on 24 September 1979. *G. S. Cutts*

LEFT One of the ways in which coaching stock was moved from carriage sidings into a station, in particular terminals, was by a propelling movement. Here we see the stock for the Paris to London sleeping cars propelled into Dover Marine to form the 7.20am to Victoria on Easter Sunday, 18 April 1954. *N. W. Sprinks*

trains into the station from carriage sheds situated at both ends of a station helped at peak periods, by reducing platform occupancy, but if they were too far away they increased the necessity of occupying the main running lines for empty stock workings.

Station pilots are perhaps more common on model railways than on the prototype, so a brief examination of some of their duties may be useful (*see* Chapter 6 for further reference). The railway companies were conscious of shunting costs and, if possible, would use a train engine to undertake shunting duties rather than to employ a dedicated shunting engine, this being particularly true of the larger passenger stations.

Where it was necessary to employ a station pilot, this particular locomotive could have varying duties – for example, the two sides of Birmingham New Street each had their own pilot as, prior to 1923, it had been a joint LNWR and Midland station, but after 1923 it was operated by two separate divisions (Western and Midland). The station pilots on the old LNWR side (which later became the LMS Western Division) were tank engines that were used as shunters, moving carriages and adding or detaching vehicles, but on the Midland Division side the west pilot was a passenger tender engine whose additional duty was to assist a westbound express passenger train by banking it on the rising gradient through the tunnels at the west end of the station and, if required, to act as train pilot to an express passenger train as far away as Gloucester. Most of its time was spent doing nothing, although any carriage movements between platforms and sidings, together with shunting in the Fish Dock Sidings on the west side of the station, were among its duties.

There were numerous locations on the British railway system where large tender engines were retained to either assist as a pilot engine or, in an emergency, to take over the working of an express train. In reality they spent most of their time doing nothing other than moving a few carriages around when required. Station pilots were also used to attach or detach dining, mail, parcels and sleeping carriages, and to assist when trains were divided or combined, this work being largely undertaken at junction stations. Sometimes pilots drew the stock into stations, mainly terminals, with the train engine attached to the rear. When uncoupled, the engine that had drawn the carriages into the station could assist by banking at what was now the rear of the train.

Summary

Locomotives to work passenger trains could arrive at the departure station either coupled to the train, as a light engine direct from the engine shed, or as part of a train that had terminated at the station and been worked forward by another engine. Light engines were sometimes coupled together to save a block. Carriages could be disposed via shunting them at the station either into a siding or a platform, working them away to carriage sidings or a carriage shed or working them forward as empty coaching stock to another station, to take up a loaded train working.

(I have omitted to mention 'turn-back trains', which is a railway term for a passenger train that arrives at a station and terminates, whereupon the engine runs round and then works the same train back again. See pp52-55 of *Railway Operation for the Modeller*.)

ABOVE There was a right and a wrong way to couple an engine to carriages. The sequence for coupling was: first, the screw coupling; second, the vacuum or Westinghouse pipe; finally, if it was within the carriage warming season, the train heating pipes and then the cocks were opened. When the reverse sequence began, the shunter had to turn off the steam-cocks before separating the steam-heating pipes. This picture was taken for a staff training book in order to show what happened if you didn't turn off the cocks. *British Railways*

ABOVE RIGHT Most of the passenger train services on the Evesham line were worked from Birmingham New Street to Ashchurch and return, but some trains from Birmingham terminated at Evesham. The engine ran round and the train stood in one of the sidings until it was time to return to the platform. In this early 1960s picture, we see Ivatt 2-6-0 No 43046 about to move the stock back to the up platform. The picture suggests that the engine has just buffered up to the coaches and is being coupled before the forward move can take place. *M. Mensing*

ABOVE A 'mixed train' ran under passenger train headlamp code, conveying passengers in carriages behind the engine with additional goods wagons behind the coaches and a brakevan at the rear. They were a feature of branch line working for many years and the subject is covered in *Railway Operation for the Modeller*. During the course of the journey, this train would detach and attach the wagons. As far as I can recall, I have never seen a mixed train run on a model railway. This undated picture from *circa* 1928 shows an ex-Highland Railway 4-4-0T running as LMS No 15013, working a mixed train. *A. G. Ellis*

LEFT Attaching and detaching carriages and non-passenger carrying stock vehicles at large stations was commonplace. Photographed at Plymouth on 1 November 1960, this picture shows a six-wheel milk-tank wagon being attached to or detached from the rear of a passenger train. A GWR 2-6-2T No 5511 is the shunt engine.

Both tank and tender engines were used to move empty carriages between the stations and carriage sidings. In this 11 February 1958 picture taken at Clapham Junction carriage siding, we see a Southern 0-6-2T locomotive No 32560 at the head of an empty carriage train. *Peter Tatlow*

ABOVE Running under shunting engine headlamp code (enabling railwaymen, in particular signalmen, to know what train was approaching), this 21 July 1959 view was taken at Inverness and shows ex Caledonian 0-4-4T No 55236 with a train of empty coaching stock. *Peter Tatlow*

LEFT Many major stations had one or more sidings between the platforms where stock was held. Sometimes, it was a complete train but it could be a single vehicle or locomotive. In this picture, taken at Plymouth on 18 July 1959, there appear to be at least two vehicles that will be attached to a train in due course.

LEFT This mixed train hauled by ex-Caledonian 0-4-4T No 15215 was taken *c*1928 and provides a good idea of the modelling potential for mixed trains, with an interesting mixture of carriages, two open goods wagons and a passenger brakevan in the rear. (Unfortunately, as stated, I have never been able to find a picture of a mixed train engaged in shunting.)

RIGHT The station pilot in this picture, taken at Carlisle on 26 July 1986, is Class 08 No 08808, seen with two Intercity Motorail vans on one of the centre roads between the platforms. Twenty-five years earlier, the most likely engine to carry out this duty would have been an LMS Standard Class 3F 0-6-0T. *W. A. Sharman*

LEFT CENTRE LEFT Displaying shunting engine headlamp code, this undated view of No 46500 shows the locomotive engaged in shunting work at a location unknown to the author.

LEFT CENTRE RIGHT On 29 October 1974, Class 03 No 03086 waits at Norwich station to draw the empty carriages that formed an express passenger train from Liverpool Street. However, until all the parcels have been unloaded the move cannot take place. *J. C. Hillmer*

RIGHT Photographed at Callington on 15 August 1964, No 41206 is at the end of its last passenger train working of the day, preparing to move the carriages to where they will stand overnight until required tomorrow or the following day. *Michael P. Jacobs*

LEFT BELOW LEFT As we have seen, the countrywide parcels services provide the modeller with opportunities. This picture was taken at Liverpool Street on 12 June 1966 and shows men loading 'BRUTE' (British Railways Universal Trolley Equipment) trolleys into an express parcels van. The vehicles that were added to or detached from parcels trains came from feeder services, or were detached to join feeder services, at numerous points across the country. See page 43 for an example of how widespread the connections were. *British Railways*

RIGHT End loading docks were found at many stations, both through and terminals. Usually they were part of the station itself, but sometimes they were a separate structure. At King's Cross on 8 May 1988, we see cars being unloaded off the 20.25 SO Aberdeen to King's Cross sleeper. Non-passenger coaching-stock vehicles with end-loading facilities were in service from the early 1900s, but the need to shunt the vehicle against the end of the dock remained a constant feature of railway operation. *A. A. J. Proctor*

LEFT The rolling stock used on parcels trains varied. At Wolverhampton Low Level on 7 May 1963, we can see covered goods vans with a passenger brakevan in the background. It is not clear exactly where this was at the station, but it was usual to use bay platforms for loading purposes. The empty vehicles would be placed in the bays by the shunting engine and then, at the appointed time, either added to a train that had arrived or form a train to be worked away. *Ian Allan Library*

ABOVE Cairnie Junction, 21 July 1959. 2-6-0 No 76104 has just arrived with the 9.35am from Elgin via Craigellachie, uncoupled and drawn forward to allow the 9.30 from Elgin via the costal route to be attached before the combined train proceeds to Aberdeen. *Peter Tatlow*

RIGHT Class 08 No 08827 is seen hauling the empty stock out of the arrival platform at Perth. Although taken on 29 August 1985, this photo's only real difference from the steam era is that a diesel shunter has replaced a steam locomotive. *W. A. Sharman*

BELOW RIGHT This is probably a train engine which has run round the train, but there are no headlamps on the tender and the door of the van is open! The man in the picture, probably a shunter, appears to be trying to enter the carriage. It is not clear if the van is being attached or detached. The picture was taken at Mallaig on 12 July 1958 and is described as 'shunting empty coaching stock'; the locomotive is 2-6-0 No 61789. *Peter Tatlow*

RIGHT 0-6-0T No 47492 shunting carriages at Carlisle, 10 September 1960. Note the headlamp over each buffer; it should be the same at the bunker end of the locomotive. *D. P. Rowland*

BELOW This picture, taken during the pre-1923 period, shows the unchanging stance of the passenger train guard giving the 'right away'. He stood still, held the green flag steady and blew his whistle. If the platform was curved and the driver could not see the guard, one or more of the station staff would repeat the signal. As the train began to move, the guard would jump into the carriage.

RIGHT To illustrate how the LMS set out the details of train formation, I have taken three examples from the Central Division Passenger Train Marshalling Arrangements dated May 2 1938 Until Further Notice. *(Top)* This shows the composition of the 9.43am from Liverpool Exchange to Preston Saturday-excepted service. There were two sections – one for Glasgow the other for Edinburgh – and at Preston the train was combined with the 9.35am Manchester to Carlisle, at which point further train marshalling would take place. *(Centre)* This is an example of a parcels train that departed from Manchester Victoria for Normanton at 8.45pm. Note how, during the journey, vehicles were attached and detached. *(Below)* The 5.22pm Manchester Victoria to Southport shows that not all passenger trains were subjected to re-marshalling en route; apart from the addition of the composite on two days of the week, the formation was not altered.

Marshalling		Balance
9-43 a.m. LIVERPOOL (Exchange) to PRESTON SX. (Class "A" stock.)		
Third Brake		
Compo	Glasgow—	9 5 a.m.
Third Vestibule		
First Restaurant Car		
Compo	Edinburgh—	9 5 a.m.
Third Brake		
Attached Preston to 9.35 a.m. Manchester (V.) to Carlisle.		
Tonnage—200.		

Marshalling		Balance
8-45 p.m. MANCHESTER (Victoria) to NORMANTON S. (Parcels train)		
a Parcel Van	—Doncaster	2025
b Brake Van	—Newcastle	2130
Compo Brake	Normanton	915
Brake Van		2017, 2138
Attach rear of Newcastle van at Rochdale.		
bc Brake Van	—Liverpool (Ex.)	
	Newcastle..	2046
c Brake Van	—Liverpool (Ex.)	
	Normanton..	2045
a Detached Wakefield and forward 5-45 a.m.		
b Forward 11-42 p.m. from Normanton.		
c Received off 6-37 p.m. ex Liverpool (Exchange).		
Tonnage—80 to Rochdale. **120 Rochdale to Wakefield.** **110 from Wakefield.**		

5-22 p.m. MANCHESTER (Victoria) to SOUTHPORT S. (Corridor stock)		
Third Brake		
Third		
Compo **MTO**		7 52 a.m.
3 Firsts		
Third		
Third Brake		
Tonnage—230 MTO, 200 MT.		

4.50 p.m. (SO), CREWE TO WHITEHAVEN. (Commences May 12th.)		
B Narrow Corridor Set (4 vehicles)	Crewe Whitehaven	160
a Third (42)	Euston Whitehaven	
a First Brake	Euston	
a Third	—Euston Barrow	
b Composite	Crewe Morecambe	
b Third Brake		246
a Received off 1.35 p.m. from Euston.		
b Transferred Preston to 5.48 p.m., Liverpool (Ex.) to Morecambe.		
B Commences May 19th.		
Tonnage—250 Crewe **195 Preston** 110 tons less on May 12th.		

2.15 p.m., CREWE TO CHESTER. (Except Saturdays commencing May 19th.) (Leaves at 2.21 p.m. on May 18th.)		
ab Third Brake	Euston Llandudno	
ab Composite	Euston Llandudno	
Bac Third (FO)		
Dac H. M. & L. Set (2 vehicles)	Birmingham Llandudno	
Ca Two Thirds	—Crewe Llandudno	
a Transferred Chester to 3.2 p.m. to Holyhead (FS), to 1.42 p.m., Liverpool to Llandudno (FO), and to 1.40 p.m., Manchester (Ex.) to Llandudno, on May 5th and 12th.		
b Received off 10.40 a.m. from Euston.		
c Received off 12.10 p.m. from Birmingham.		
B Commences May 25th.		
C May 18th only.		
D Except May 18th.		
Tonnage—110 until May 24th. **110 (F), 138 (FO) commencing May 25th.**		

ABOVE Both these examples are taken from the LMS Western Division Passenger Train Marshalling Arrangements dated April 30 1934 Until Further Notice. *(Top)* This train comprises a Crewe to Whitehaven set, two coaches from Euston to Whitehaven and finally a third-class carriage from Euston to Barrow plus two coaches from Crewe to Morecambe via Liverpool Exchange. *(Below)* The second example is a Crewe to Chester train with carriages from Euston and Birmingham to Llandudno. In both instances re-marshalling would have taken place during the journey, which provides potential for modellers. Further examples may be found in *Passenger Train Operation for the Railway Modeller* and *Railway Operation for the Modeller*.

4 Shunting and marshalling freight trains

The British railway system evolved and developed during the 19th century, probably reaching its peak about 1914. Although intense competition during the late Victorian era was supplanted by co-operation between a number of companies during the early 20th century, too many competing lines had been built, resulting in a duplication of facilities. From a modeller's point of view, however, the variety offered by the grouping and (particularly) pre-grouping periods is far better than the popular 1960-70s period, when the railway system was in decline.

I mention this simply to explain to readers unfamiliar with pre-1960s practice how the movement of traffic across the UK might seem rather unusual to those used to modern traffic flows – for example, sending traffic from East London to South Wales via Stafford, as described in Chapter 1. The reason for this is simply because the pre-group companies set their own patterns for traffic flows by using routes that they owned, which due to line occupation often continued throughout the 'big four' years and on into the BR period.

At this point it may be useful to define what is meant by 'traffic'. Broadly speaking, it was 'passenger traffic' (covered in Chapter 3) and 'goods traffic', later referred to as 'merchandise traffic'. In *The Hand-Book of Railway Stations*, published in conjunction with the Railway Clearing House in 1931, it was stated, 'Merchandise traffic means and includes all traffic carried by goods, live stock or mineral

trains,' and this classification continued to be used – although later the word 'freight' often replaced 'goods' to describe non-mineral or livestock traffic.

Although their precise titles varied, goods agents were responsible for the system of working the goods stations, including arrangements for the warehouses, shed and sidings and the loading and forwarding of all traffic by the proper trains to avoid unnecessary shunting and delays. Wagons were first examined for defects and – depending upon what had been carried on the previous trip – cleaned before being loaded. Every endeavour was made to load wagons to full capacity. Loaded wagons were then labelled to show the route, the destination and, if it was a wagonload, the owners. It was not normal practice to label empty wagons, but when this happened it was the same basic arrangement. This was because privately owned and

non-common-user wagons often had painted instructions – 'Empty to XYZ colliery' or 'Empty to XYZ junction, GWR' – which would be sufficient on their own, while, before the 'pooling' of certain vehicle types, railway company-owned wagons would be returned empty via their nearest exchange sidings. After the pooling of wagons – which happened gradually and was never universal until BR days – certain yards in an area would be collecting points for certain types of pooled wagon from whence the department in control would distribute them as required on a day-by-day basis, irrespective of who owned them.

The key to the movement of goods traffic on British railways was the marshalling yards and goods stations that were to be found across the railway system. Goods stations were the terminal point for traffic that was either loaded or unloaded, depending upon whether it was

LEFT Bridge Street goods yard at Bradford in 1956, with an unidentified ex-L&YR 0-6-0. The locomotive is propelling the train as the driver stares ahead with his hand on the locomotive brake handle; the fireman is taking life easy. Note the 'stopping freight train' headlamp code above the right-hand buffer. *B. C. Lane*

RIGHT Millions of tons of coal came into London each year by sea. The rail transit was from northern collieries to the port where it was loaded and from the London docks to its final destination, the long haul being by coastal steamer. This picture was taken at the old LB&SCR wharf at Deptford, on the south side of the River Thames, on 28 February 1940. Note that there is not a locomotive in sight, but plenty of capstans and bollards to move empty wagons alongside the collier for loading and to move them away again after. *Southern Railway*

originating or terminating. They could be very large and comprised an open yard where bulk loads (including coal) were dealt with, goods sheds where the goods passed over the deck between road and rail, and warehouses for the storage of goods in transit. Others could be quite small and only comprised one or two sidings with no shed. *The Hand-Book of Railway Stations* listed the facilities at each station, together with the private sidings.

The essential business of a goods station was to transfer goods from road vehicles to rail wagons, or vice versa, as soon as possible. To assist the movement of wagons in the sheds and yards, considerable use was made of various types of capstans, as described in the Introduction. (See the drawing on page 17 which shows how a loop capstan was able to move wagons alongside the deck inside a covered shed.) The method of working the various types of capstans varied. The 'fixed head' type employed a wire cable; one end

was secured to the capstan drum and the other end was fitted with a hook attached to the wagon(s). Depending upon local circumstances they were driven by electricity, hydraulic power or steam, and controlled by foot pedal in their many different variations.

Warehouses were an important part of many goods stations. Warehousing was a service provided by the railway companies for bulk traffic such as grain, raw cotton, wool, yarn, leather, flax, jute and 'wine and spirits', in a bonded store. At the larger stations extensive warehouses – some four or five storeys high – were built, while at small stations in agricultural areas they could be a single

storey. Regardless of size, loaded wagons had to be shunted into position for unloading, while loading required empty wagons.

The goods yard was the uncovered portion of a goods station. The major part of the operation in the yard was connected with the traffic in bulk, e.g. coal, timber, bricks, cement, lime, sand, steel girders, scrap iron and what was known as 'S to S' (station to station) traffic, in transfer between road and rail transport without the use of decks or platforms. Commodities such as the above were usually conveyed in one or more wagons and did not require sorting. Of course, not all goods yards catered for all of the above; regular loads of steel girders at a small country branch station would have been out of place, whereas coal traffic was found at most yards. In smaller yards, one or two sidings may have provided

LEFT Transhipment was an important feature in the movement of goods traffic. A large proportion of merchandise traffic was made up of miscellaneous consignments to a variety of destinations. The main traffic flows were between large towns and the volume made it both practicable and economic to schedule direct services between such places on a daily basis. However, to convey sundry traffic in small quantities in direct wagons was not always justified and transhipment at an intermediate station became necessary. In effect, small consignments were taken to depots where loads for particular destinations were consolidated, thus ensuring an economic loading for the wagons. These depots were known as tranship stations, where shunting wagons to and from the decks where traffic was consolidated took place. This picture was taken at Derby St Mary's transhipment shed on 29 March 1911, but it would have been a similar scene 25 or more years later. *NMR DY 9487*

ABOVE This undated but pre-1923 picture shows the expanse of the old Great Northern marshalling yard at Hornsey, where the four locomotives in the yard are all tank engines. *Locomotive Publishing Co*

sufficient space for unloading coal, with adjacent areas for storage. But at larger stations a separate coal yard or coal wharf was required, which was usually well away from the area used for general merchandise traffic. In coal mining areas, coal for local use was often sold at collieries on land-sale sites, and so the amount of coal traffic in the goods yard could vary. But if the colliery specialised in coal for gasworks, or produced only anthracite, then other types of coal would be brought in by rail.

It was important that shunting operations during the working day did not disturb wagons on the sidings allocated for coal discharge. The usual practice was to set the sidings with loaded wagons each morning and for them to be shunted or 'dressed' (a common term used to describe the removal of empty wagons) at the end of the day, leaving the fully or partially loaded wagons available to coal merchants for the next day.

Other aspects of the yard – where wagons had to be shunted into position for loading or unloading – included sidings, where rail vehicles could be placed undisturbed by shunting or other train movements and cart-ways allowed road vehicles alongside the rail wagons. The quantities and types of traffic and the land available determined the layout of the yard. Cranes were found at some goods stations, although their size varied. There was also a considerable traffic in the conveyance of bulk liquids – such as petrol, petroleum, ammonia, tar, creosote, etc – in tank wagons, for which special arrangements for loading and unloading were often required. Shunting these wagons into the right place remained necessary, however. Generally, the provision of empty wagons for outwards traffic came via those which had been unloaded. However, at times a special type of wagon was required and would have been ordered in advance, arriving as an empty vehicle before being shunted to its loading point.

In the United Kingdom, the bulk of goods traffic was dealt with at large town goods stations, but for modellers the small stations in country districts or on the outskirts of large towns make a more realisable option. In country districts, goods were brought to the stations by the senders or carting agents rather than by railway company cartage teams, which was the usual arrangement in towns and cities. While some large goods stations were close to marshalling yards, others were not and loaded wagons had to be taken to one before becoming part of a train and being worked towards their destination. Another factor to be considered was transhipping. There was an obvious financial desire to maximise the load carried in each wagon, which was achieved by sending small consignments to one of the transhipping points on the line. (The subject is covered in the

LEFT Birmingham Central goods station dealt with coal and goods traffic and was served by both local trip workings, as well as being the terminal for originating and terminating freight trains. This picture was taken on 26 September 1922, looking towards the centre of Birmingham. To the right we can see part of the main goods shed with the warehouse above, while to the left is the copper shed where the 0-6-0T is shunting wagons.

RIGHT This c1918 picture was taken at the L&SWR yard at Nine Elms and shows one end of the marshalling yard fenced off from the electrified main lines. *'Topical' Press Agency Ltd*

railway companies' *General Directions to Agents and Members of Their Staffs, Management of Stations and Conveyance of Merchandise Traffic.*) Shunting these wagons – including the road and tariff vans which carried many of the combined loads – is a factor to consider for modellers with small stations or those who wish to include this element in their working practices.

A large amount of rail-borne traffic originated from or was taken to private sidings, where employees of the sender loaded into or unloaded from rail vehicles. In many instances, the character of the traffic was such that no other arrangement would be practical and the layout of the works was designed accordingly. Private sidings were connected to the railway company's lines and, depending upon size, the private company could have their own locomotives to carry out internal shunting while the railway company locomotive would just detach incoming and attach outgoing traffic. Otherwise, the railway company locomotive undertook whatever internal shunting was required. (Further examples of private sidings can be found in *Freight Train Operation for the Railway Modeller.*)

For a full understanding of freight train working and shunting it is important to understand the nature and function of marshalling yards. Throughout the United Kingdom, wagons were loaded at thousands

of different points for delivery to thousands of different destinations, but this could only be achieved by association with other wagons that shared part of the journey.

For example, let us consider a wagon loaded at a small station near Aberdeen and consigned to a similar station near York. A local working, often referred to as a pickup freight, would run along the branch detaching wagons with traffic for stations along the line and attaching wagons that had been loaded with outwards traffic, plus any empty wagons that had been unloaded. At the Aberdeen marshalling yard,

this wagon would be shunted into a siding together with others to form a trainload for a yard near Edinburgh, where the train would be broken up and individual wagons (or groups of wagons for the same destinations) shunted into various sidings. Our wagon would go into a siding reserved for York traffic; such was the volume of traffic for York from Edinburgh that a full trainload could be assembled without use of intermediate yards. On arrival at York, our wagon would be shunted into a siding allocated to traffic for the branch on which the destination station was located. It would travel from York as part of a pickup goods train for that branch, along with wagons from all over the country that had arrived at York by similar means.

Marshalling yards were necessary to enable single wagons or groups of wagons to be concentrated into trains. The traffic may have originated locally or it may have been received from other yards a long way off, perhaps on another railway or – after 1948 – from another region of the nationalised system. The first function carried out at a marshalling yard was to form the traffic produced by the breaking up and reforming of other trains received from elsewhere into new trains. The other was to disperse over the immediate vicinity any local traffic which had arrived in those trains. Although prototype marshalling yards were generally larger than most modellers can reproduce, there are exceptions. During World War Two, a fan of six sidings at Kings Norton adjacent to the carriage sidings was used as relief sidings for Washwood Heath marshalling yard; this allowed some trains that came into the Birmingham area with what

·	·	·	·	·	·	·	·	Church Siding	Essex	L. N. E. (G. E.)	See Tolleshunt D'Arcy.
								Church Street Coal Depôt	Yorks	H. & O. Jt. (L. N. E. (G.N.) & L.M.S. (L.&Y.))	See Halifax.
G	P	F	L	H	C		2 10	Church Stretton	Salop	S. & H. Jt. (G. W. & L. M. S. (L. N. W.))	Craven Arms and Shrewsbury.
	P							Churchtown	Lancs	L. M. S. (L. & Y.)	Preston and Southport.
	P*							Church Village Halt	Glamorg'n	G. W. (T. V.)	Treforest and Llantwit Fardre.
G	·	F						Churn	Berks	G. W.	Didcot and Newbury.
	P*							‡Churn Halt	Berks	G. W.	Upton and Compton.
								Churnet Valley Gas Co.'s Sid.	Staffs	L. M. S. (N. S.)	Kingsley & Froghall.
								Churn Lane Siding	Kent	Southern (S. E. C.)	Horsmonden.
G	P	F	L	H	C		3 0	Churston Station & Junction	Devon	G. W.	Kingswear and Torquay.
	P							Churwell	Yorks	L. M. S. (L. N. W.)	Dewsbury and Leeds.
G	P		L	H				Chwilog	Caernarvn	L. M. S. (L. N. W.)	Afon Wen and Caernarvon.
								Cilely Collieries, Ltd., Cilely Colliery	Glamorg'n	G. W.	Tonyrefail.
								Cilely Colliery	Glamorg'n	G. W.	Same as Cilely Collieries, Ltd. (Tonyrefail).

NOTES.
STATION ACCOMMODATION.
The following is an Explanation of the letters used throughout the Book to indicate the Station Accommodation :—

G	...	Goods Station.
G*	...	Coal Class, Mineral and S. to S. Traffic in Truck Loads.
P	...	Passenger and Parcel Station.
P*	...	Passenger, but not Parcel or Miscellaneous Traffic.
P†	...	Parcel and Miscellaneous Traffic only.
F	...	Furniture Vans, Carriages, Motor Cars, Portable Engines, and Machines on Wheels.
L	...	Live Stock.
H	...	Horse Boxes and Prize Cattle Vans.
C	...	Carriages and Motor Cars by Passenger Train.

CRANE POWER.
The Crane Power shown represents the maximum *fixed* crane power at each Station, but most of the Companies have travelling cranes with a lifting power of five tons and upwards, which can be removed from one Station to another, as circumstances require.

ABOVE AND LEFT The Railway Clearing House fulfilled many functions for the British railway companies, including the production at regular intervals of a Hand-Book of Railway Stations. The notes *(left)* clearly show the various categories of train that each siding could accommodate.

This small section of the 1938 edition *(above)* shows a variety of locations with all the listed station accommodation, passenger stations with/without parcels and private sidings. (Also note the use of the term 'goods station', not 'goods yard'.)

RIGHT Photographed on 14 October 1962, this shows an ex-Midland Railway 0-6-0T No 41875 shunting at Staveley Old Works. *Paul Cotterell*

TOP LEFT Dewsnap sidings were on the Woodhead line near Guide Bridge and were an important marshalling yard for freight traffic. This picture shows the first cut from the train that was to be shunted; the brakevan was rolling towards the No 1 group of sorting sidings. *G. Richard Parkes Collection*

LEFT TOP RIGHT This overall view of the new marshalling yard at Tinsley was taken from the control tower when shunting was in progress. The advantages of a modern yard can be seen: plenty of lighting and no need for shunters to chase the wagons to apply the brakes and slow them down; this is done by the retarders. *British Railways*

LEFT CENTRE LEFT In this undated picture taken at Dewsnap sidings (c1960), we can see a train on No 1 Reception Road waiting for a yard pilot to move it to where it will be broken up and shunted into sidings, according to destination. We can also see an electric Class EM1 Bo-Bo at the head of a train, ready to leave the yard, while the yard inspector keeps his eye on the time to ensure there will not be any late departures. *G. Richard Parkes Collection*

LEFT CENTRE RIGHT The hump at the marshalling yard at Feltham on the old Southern Railway is seen in this c1950 picture, with shunting in progress. No railwaymen can be seen as a group visiting the shed and yard look on. *Ian Allan Library*

LEFT BELOW The marshalling yard at Bescot, near Walsall on the old LNWR, was modernised during the 1960s. This picture, taken on 4 May 1966, shows the extent of the yard. During the steam era there was a large locomotive depot at Bescot. The photograph was taken from the top of an office block, looking south across the down sorting sidings towards the up sidings. *British Railways*

were described as 'rough wests' (i.e. a westbound train not shunted into station order) to terminate at Kings Norton, where the wagons (usually coal traffic) were shunted to form trains for a variety of destinations beyond Birmingham (e.g. Gloucester, Worcester, Cheltenham or Bristol). Therefore, while most of the shunting of wagons to form trains was largely carried out at the major yards, there were many exceptions (in particular private sidings) which offer potential modelling opportunities. Also offering potential for modellers are the junctions between two branches where traffic from Branch A was detached and left in a siding to be collected by an engine working along Branch B, or vice versa.

The work of the yardmaster, inspector and their staff was to marshal the wagons for forward despatch, for which it was usual to allocate sidings for traffic to specific destinations.

As we have seen, some marshalling yards received most of their traffic from other yards that were some distance away, while large goods stations with adjacent marshalling yards received traffic that had been loaded there as well as traffic from other goods yards in the area. It was not unusual to have first and second sorting operations, where the layout of the yard allowed it. Wagons for stations along a particular route would be shunted onto one siding and then shunted again into station order later, using other short sidings. The classic arrangement is: 1) the reception sidings where trains arrive; 2) marshalling sidings where wagons are shunted to form new trains; 3) second sorting sidings where the wagons are shunted into station order; 4) departure sidings. However, many marshalling yards comprised reception and sorting sidings only, with the complete train departing from the sorting siding which was also the departure siding. This latter arrangement is more suited to most modellers.

One of the most time-wasting features of shunting was dealing with private owners' wagons and wagons belonging to other railway companies, whose stock was described as 'foreign'. This subject has been covered in *Freight Train Operation for the Railway Modeller*, but brief comment is called for. Prior to 1915, all foreign

LEFT This undated picture shows an old North Eastern Railway Class P1 (LNER Class J25), now running as British Railways No 65706, after propelling a string of wagons for discharging into the ships along the new concrete deck on West Blyth staithes. When the wagons have been emptied they will run by gravity down the track on the left side of the train. *J. D. Smith*

ABOVE Many large marshalling yards had locomotive facilities. The most obvious was the supply of water for locomotives, which was commonplace, but others included turntables, ash pits where the ashpan could be raked out and inspection pits to enable the driver to inspect and oil the engine. Generally, a locomotive on a diagram that was 'out and back' would take sufficient coal at the home depot so all that was needed was to bring it forward and to clean the fire. (Some locations did have coaling facilities, usually for tank engines whose supply of coal was limited.) In this picture – exact location unknown, somewhere in the London area – the locomotive is a North London Railway 0-6-0T used for shunting and local freight work. It is standing alongside a coaling platform and an inspection or ash pit is just visible behind the engine.

ABOVE Severn Tunnel down marshalling yard, 13 May 1967. Shunting is in progress, with two shunters chasing the wagons to apply the handbrakes. *Frank Lawton*

stock had to be returned promptly to the owning company either as an empty or else 'back loaded' with traffic. In 1915, there were the first agreements between companies to treat some stock as 'common user' (i.e. shared between the railway companies); however, this did not apply to private owner wagons until 1939. As a result, a lot of shunting took place to ensure foreign and private owner wagons were returned promptly, ensuring that the latter

went to the colliery that owned them while various coal factors' and merchants' empty wagons were sent to the colliery they purchased coal from. During and after World War Two, virtually all coal wagons were 'common user' and a train of empties was no longer shunted individually; it was merely a case of colliery X needed 60 empty wagons, so the next train took the first 60 that were ready to go.

Exchange sidings also provide modellers with many options for shunting. These were where traffic was exchanged between two separate organisations, i.e. between two railway companies or, after 1923, different divisions of the same company. The majority of exchange sidings were probably between railway companies and collieries where small industrial locomotives engaged in shunting and handling the internal traffic, while the railway companies' locomotive brought the inwards traffic and worked away the outwards traffic – although some shunting duties by train engines were commonplace.

There were a number of rules that governed the formation of trains. Grease axlebox wagons remained in use until the late 1950s, when wooden-bodied coal wagons were replaced by 16T steel mineral wagons, while the extinction of grease-box goods vehicles

LEFT There were many places where shunting took place alongside water, in this case over the River Severn swing bridge. Here we see a diesel shunter No D2137 engaged in shunting wagons on the old GWR Gloucester Docks branch on 23 January 1967. *W. Potter*

RIGHT This picture, location unknown, has been included to show a private siding adjacent to a station. The date on the reverse of the print is 13 July 1958 and the reason for a string of wagons on a running line is far from clear. The fact that the siding has been made unusable suggests the line may have been closed or reduced to a single line working. The important point for modellers is that private sidings – with the gate marking where the railway company maintenance ends – could be part of a station area and were not always large. Those who model the final years of steam, or the post-1968 period, may find the closed private siding with unusable rails an interesting modelling project. *M. Hale*

was probably a few years earlier. For many years, wagons with grease axleboxes were not permitted on express passenger, parcels, newspaper, fish, meat, fruit, milk, horse or perishable trains composed of coaching stock, or fitted freight trains which had the continuous brake in use on not less than one third of the vehicles. The instructions varied over the years, the particular section paraphrased above being dated 1934.

Particular care was taken with wagons conveying livestock. The wagons were placed on the train, where they would be subject to the minimum amount of shunting; wherever possible, cattle wagons fitted with automatic brakes would be coupled next to the engine with their brakes connected, while any handbrake-only cattle wagons were coupled behind the fitted vehicles. There were numerous instructions regarding the conveyance of explosives and other dangerous goods, including the requirement (until World War Two, when block trains for fuel were initiated) that no more than five vehicles containing explosives or flammable liquids should be in a train and that they should be marshalled as near to the centre of the train as possible. When shunting trains

that included this traffic, special care obviously had to be taken.

As far as freight trains were concerned, there was usually a considerable amount of shunting with stopping freight- or pickup goods trains. When the train engine arrived at the yard, there would probably not be any shunting required; however, it is possible that a vehicle (or vehicles) may have needed to be attached to the front of the train before its journey began. Although stopping freight trains were usually associated with country districts, they were to be seen at all stations with goods facilities at sometime during the day. One particular exception was rural branch lines (or ends of branch lines), which in latter years may have seen freight trains only once or twice a week, but most lines retained a daily goods train into the 1960s or 70s, even if it no longer needed to stop at every station. Many stations in the inner cities did not have goods

facilities and were passenger- or passenger-and-parcel-traffic-only, but while passenger traffic only also applied to a number of halts, the majority of passenger stations dealt with goods and mineral traffic. Depending upon size and location, these stations saw one or more stopping freight trains each day and the diagrammed working included the train engine shunting the sidings before departure to the next stopping place.

Tow-roping

On models hump shunting is not very easy, but tow-roping is more easily reproduced. With the exception of places that were authorised, the movement of vehicles by towing with a rope attached to the locomotive (or another vehicle) was prohibited. Rule 110(c) of the *Railway Companies Rule Book* states: 'The movement of vehicles by means of a prop or pole, or by towing with a rope or chain attached to an engine or vehicle moving on an adjacent line, is strictly prohibited, except where specially authorised by the Chief Operating Manager.' The sectional appendix states, 'The man engaged in the operation must not stand or walk in advance of the rope, but must, in all cases, take care to place himself in the rear of the rope to avoid any risk of injury in case it should break or become detached. The number of vehicles to be moved by a tow rope at one time must be regulated by the weight of the loads they

LEFT Wicker goods station in Sheffield was surrounded by either factories or houses. As we can see, there are separate fans of siding and in the centre of the picture there are capstans to enable wagons to be shunted without using horses or locomotives. Photographed on 13 May 1912, the livery of rolling stock and the addition of motor road vehicles would be the most visible changes 40 years later, by which time almost no horses were used. *NRM DY 1697*

ABOVE An unusual but very useful feature for modellers who want something different is the use of wagon turntables for shunting traffic at some roadside stations. The stations in question were on the old Midland Railway Gloucester to Bristol line – although there may have been similar arrangements elsewhere in Great Britain. In this undated south-facing picture of Charfield, the wagon turntable has trailing connections from both the up and down running lines which were protected by catch points. There was a short siding into the goods shed and the side loading dock. A van is visible on a third siding but there were two more short sidings to the left, hidden by the goods shed.

contain, the gradient of the line and other circumstances, and care must be taken that no greater number of vehicles is moved at one time than can be towed with safety.'

At the other end of the scale, express freight trains also stopped en route to detach or attach traffic. These stops were quite brief; the train would stop and the train engine would draw off the wagons to be detached. These vehicles could be 'on the engine', which meant they were coupled to the tender, or else coupled

'behind X', which meant a given number of wagons were coupled to the engine and would remain part of the train. The train engine undertook these shunting moves, although the local shunt engine would have set any wagons to be attached and later moved the wagons that had been detached.

During these stops it was usual for the train engine to take water, the wagons in the train to be examined and maybe the engine crew to be changed. These moves could take place within a yard, but also when the train was on a goods line adjacent to sidings or even on the main line, provided sufficient time was available between scheduled trains.

Finally, we must not overlook what some railwaymen would call 'being put inside'. This was a regular occurrence for goods trains that were running late and risking delaying a faster or more important train. If they did not have enough time to reach a point where they could be overtaken, a goods loop or their destination, then the signalman would bring the train to a stand so that it could be set back into a refuge siding (also known as a lie-bye, or lay-by in GWR terms), onto a handy branch line or even across to the opposite main line, to clear the road for a following train. Either the signalman could make this decision or he could be instructed to take action by the control office.

ABOVE It was commonplace for railway company locomotives to undertake shunting duties at private sidings where the owners did not have their own locos. These would usually be small installations as with the ex-Midland Railway 0-4-0T No 41528 in this picture, working at what I believe is an open-cast site in the Midlands. *T. G. Hepburn*

RIGHT ABOVE The use of old 0-6-0s for local trip working was commonplace. It was only during the final years of steam that modern engines, displaced by other forms of motive power, were regularly employed on light duties. This picture was taken at Harborne in July 1949, several years after the passenger service ceased, and shows an ex-LNWR 0-6-0 No 28616 shunting at the goods yard after arriving with a local freight train. *P. B. Whitehouse*

RIGHT BELOW The LMS-designed Class 2MT 2-6-0s were intended to replace old time-expired engines on secondary work. In this 27 July 1964 picture we see No 46422 engaged on shunting at Lancaster Green Ayre. *Paul Cotterell*

LEFT Many large companies owned distribution warehouses where consignments of their products arrived on a regular basis. This early 1930s picture shows No 37 trip – note the target board on the left lamp holder – at Cadbury's London depot, Finchley. The vans would have arrived at one of the London marshalling yards after travelling direct from either Birmingham Central or Lawley Street goods stations in Birmingham. Following arrival in London, the vans would have been shunted into the trip working for the depot. No 3559 is seen shunting them to where they will be unloaded. *'Topical' Press Agency Ltd*

RIGHT Although shunting was no longer taking place when this *c*1960 picture was taken, it shows part of a small goods yard at Hagley. Note how the cattle dock was placed so that an engine could attach or detach wagons while the train remained on the running line with all movements under the direct control of the signalman. There was another connection in front of the cattle dock that gave access to the siding on the left. Judging by the track formation in the bottom left-hand corner of the picture, there was another trailing connection to the other running line. Subject to timetable constraints, traffic to and from Hagley could be attached or detached while the train remained on the running lines. *J. Moss*

LEFT ABOVE LEFT During the post-war period, a number of ex-War Department locomotives were sold to private companies for use on their internal railways and sidings where they were engaged in shunting and marshalling duties. This picture was taken at Grimesthorpe colliery, Cudworth, Yorkshire in 1946. The locomotive in the centre of the picture is No 4 (previously WD No 75305) while the one to the left is No 5 (ex-WD No 75306); both were built by the Vulcan foundry in 1945. *Wakefield Collection*

LEFT ABOVE RIGHT Control of entry to and from sidings – whether railway company-owned or private – was exercised from signalboxes, but there were many places where ground frames were used. This was usually because the connection was too far from the signalbox to be worked by a mechanical lever frame, so an alternative method was employed. This was to install a lever frame that could only be used after the signalman in the nearby box unlocked the ground frame to allow either the train guard or shunter to work the levers and the train to enter the sidings or to depart. (The subject of ground frames is dealt with in *Railway Signalling and Track Plans*.) *R. S. Carpenter*

LEFT CENTRE LEFT There were many locations where trains were propelled to where the shunting would begin, rather than drawn in by a locomotive that ran around the train or another engine undertaking the shunting duties. This picture was taken during 1937 at Five Ways, Birmingham and shows No 1700 prior to propelling back into Birmingham Central goods station. Note the tail and side lamps on the brakevan. (See also p54) *P. B. Whitehouse*

LEFT CENTRE RIGHT Locomotives with short wheelbases generally carried out shunting at docks and harbours. In this 17 August 1928 view taken at Weymouth quay, we can see a small saddle tank, either No 2194 or 2195, shunting wagons during the transfer of goods to or from the steamer. *Roger Carpenter Collection*

LEFT BOTTOM In this May 1931 picture taken at Folkestone harbour, we can see 'R' class 0-6-0T No A152 engaged in shunting duties. The unusual vehicle next to the locomotive is the ex-SE&CR harbour brakevan. *Milepost 92½*

ABOVE Cattle docks were used when livestock, also including pigs and sheep, were loaded into or removed from cattle wagons and also when livestock was required to be fed or watered during the course of a journey. They were not used as storage pens for longer than necessary. The docks varied in size, but it was necessary to move the wagon alongside the gates for loading or unloading whether there was only one or 40 cattle wagons to be dealt with. (Modellers tend to have cattle in the pen as a permanent feature, which is not correct.) This picture was taken at Derby cattle dock on 26 November 1909 and shows unloading taking place. This dock could accommodate several wagons at a time. (For further reference to cattle traffic, see *Freight Train Operation for the Railway Modeller*.)

London Midland and Scottish Railway Company.
LIVE STOCK.

ABOVE The railway companies took the examination of cattle while in transit seriously and a number of regulations applied. Cattle wagons were to be marshalled in such a position to ensure the wagons underwent the minimum amount of shunting; when two or more wagons were on the same train, the couplings were to be tightly screwed up. Cattle in transit had to be watered and fed at fixed intervals; on long journeys this required the wagons to be detached from the train and put into a cattle dock.

Some shunting examples

Describing shunting in a book is not easy; the best approach would be for the reader to witness full-size locomotives and rolling stock, but this is no longer possible. What follows is based upon Edward S. Hadley's work, *The Shunter's Manual*. I have used his original text although, to provide continuity, a few alterations have been necessary. I hope that it shows the reader how railwaymen in the past dealt with shunting goods stock.

Shunting Example 1

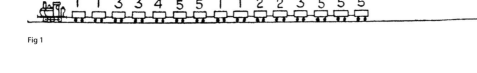

Fig 1

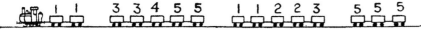

Fig 2

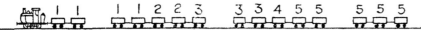

Fig 3

FIG. 1 Here are 15 'mixed' wagons. The numbers represent the destination stations, No 1 being the first to be detached and No 5 the last, so the wagons have to be marshalled into station order; the '1' is next to the engine, the '2' is next, and so on – the '5' is at the rear. The shunter would begin by assessing what was in the siding and decide how he would proceed to do the job. Now let us show the wagons again in the same order but with some divisions between them, thus:

FIG. 2 It will now be seen that by the simple process of placing the *third* section between the *first* and *second* sections, all the wagons will then stand in the order required, thus:

FIG. 3 Therefore, the quickest approach is to draw forward the wagons comprising the front three sections, shunt aside those in the *third* section, place the *second* section against the *fourth*, and then, with the *first* section on the engine, pick up the *third* (bringing the four '1's together), and back the combined *first* and *third* sections against the others.

Shunting Example 2

Fig 4

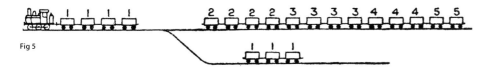
Fig 5

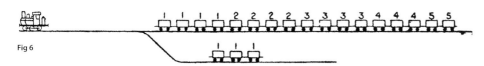
Fig 6

Here is another example – a batch of wagons with those in front of the '3's to be put into station order:

FIG. 4 Two procedures present themselves. One is to shunt aside the intermediate batch of three '1's, then to shunt the four '2's against the '3's, and finally, with four '1's on the engine, to pick up the three '1's from the siding and place all the seven '1's against the '2's, as illustrated above:

FIG. 5 However, as we can see, the '2's and the four '1's in front of them *may be regarded as a single unit*, and therefore should not be separated; and after the batch of three '1's have been shunted aside, the other '1's should be shunted off along with the '2's, leaving only the three '1's to be picked up by the light engine, thus:

FIG. 6 The difference between the two methods can be summarised as:

FIRST METHOD

No of wagons attached/detached	No conveyed
Detach 3	11
Detach 4	8
Attach 3	7
Detach 7	7
Total	**33**

SECOND METHOD

No of wagons attached/detached	No conveyed
Detach 3	11
Detach 8	8
Attach 3	3
Detach 3	3
Total	**25**

Although our sample has only 20 wagons, this shows how complex the subject can become, so it is easy to see that a train of 40 or more wagons that had to be placed into station order required skill and understanding if the work was to be accomplished in a reasonable amount of time. There were some guidelines that can be briefly summarised here:

• Do not separate wagons and, if possible, handle them as a single unit.

• Avoid 'long shunts' and use 'short shunts'. This is obvious at night or during fog, but under good weather conditions the advantages are: driver nearer to shunter and his signals more easily seen from the engine. With less wagons attached to the engine, the driver has more control and can carry out the shunting more quickly, movements are less violent and this helps to avoid damage to wagons and displacement of loads.

• Know your siding room and watch how many wagons are placed there, so that you do not overfill the space available.

• Anticipate later requirements. Be sure about destinations and use foresight when breaking up a train.

• Avoid 'long shunts' with 30 or more wagons coupled to the engine, shunting them off in '1's and '2's. This is the worst approach and doubles the work that the job demands.

• Before beginning to break up a batch of 'mixed' wagons, a shunter should particularly notice any groups of wagons that already stand in their right final order, such as where '1's are next to '2's, '2's next to '3's, and so on. Obviously it would be folly to uncouple and separate any such companion wagons if it were practicable to handle the combination as a single unit. Shunters should acquire the ability to perceive what adjoining wagons comprise groups that may be left intact. A shunter who will take the pains to be observant will find that this ability will soon 'grow upon him' from his day-to-day experience.

LEFT This picture was taken in July 1949 and shows an ex-Midland Railway double frame 0-6-0 No 22846 shunting at Halesowen. The locomotive had arrived with a local freight train and would depart with traffic that had originated at Halesowen together with any empties that were not required. *P. B. Whitehouse*

Shunting Example 3

We continue with an example that could be entitled 'Marshalling in a Restricted Space' and could have been written with 21st-century railway modellers in mind. When traffic is light and there is ample siding room, the operations of shunting and marshalling are quite straightforward; but when the conditions are otherwise, the quality of the work depends upon the shunter's expertness and resource. Exceptionally heavy traffic inflicts upon the shunter a two-fold disadvantage. Not only are there a greater number of wagons to be handled, but also in the handling of them he is hampered by curtailed siding room and restricted working space.

At ordinary times it is, of course, advantageous to achieve economies in time and wagon movements – to use light and short-cut ways of doing the work; but when the traffic is superabundant and the available siding room is meagre, great benefit attaches to those methods that require only a minimum of space, movements, and time. Some shunters, owing to inadequate experience, assume that each siding affords room, in the sorting process, for wagons for only one destination, and they proceed to do the work accordingly. This is unfortunate, because they deny themselves one of the most expeditious methods of getting the wagons into station order and of avoiding

needlessly 'long' shunts and this approach could apply to many modellers. With two sidings available, a shunter has at least six marshalling positions for the wagons.

FIG 1 The positions A and B are obvious. Fig. 2 shows how wagons for a second, or even a third destination, may be marshalled in either of these sidings, and how the positions E (on the train road) and F (next to the engine) may be used in the six-featured plan of operations. It will be perceived that upon backing the engine and its wagons against the wagons in A, picking these up, afterwards picking up those in B, and finally placing all against those on the train road, the whole of the wagons will be in station order.

FIG 2 For a good foundation, it is often well to begin with alternate destinations (e.g. 4 and 2, or 5 and 3) in the respective sidings, and to shunt back temporarily on to their original road, or work next to the engine, the wagons for destinations, 5, 3 and 1 in the one case, or for 4, 2 and 1 in the other case, to be shunted later against the wagons in the sidings or, if more convenient, to be marshalled separately.

The plan of working certain wagons into position F (next to the engine) is a useful one. It is accomplished in either one of two ways, or partly in both. First, cut off immediately in front of the first of these particular wagons on the train, so that for the next cut-off the engine will be attached to this wagon; then cut off immediately in front of the next of these wagons, and when the intervening wagons have been disposed of, keep the first one on the engine and bring it against the second one; and continue in this way as far as necessary. For example, if it were desired to work the '1's next to the engine, the cuts-off in this train would be as shown by the arrows in Fig 3.

FIG 3 The second plan is to shunt the particular wagons aside as they are come to and thus accumulate them together until it is convenient for the engine to be attached to them.

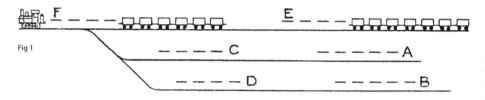

Fig 1

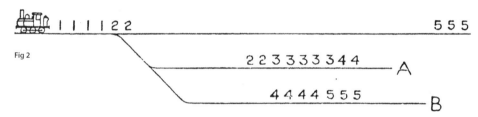

Fig 2

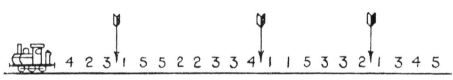

Fig 3

Shunting Example 4

This example could be described as an orthodox approach and is a rather different method of marshalling from that given so far. The work to be performed is precisely the same, namely, to put into station order the 30 'mixed' wagons for five destinations, and with only two sidings available it is in keeping with many model railways. We shall proceed in the strictly orthodox fashion of placing the '5's and '4's into one siding, the '3's and '2's into the other, and of working the '1's into the position next to the engine. The train is shown below, and the arrow indicates the place of the first cut-off.

Fig 1

FIG. 1 By cutting off here, the first two shunts (3-3 and 5) will give us the 'foundation' wagons for the two sidings, and the load on the engine (16 wagons) is not excessive. We shunt off the wagons as they come, putting all except the '3's and '5's back on to the train road. This work, when completed, gives the position shown in Fig 2.

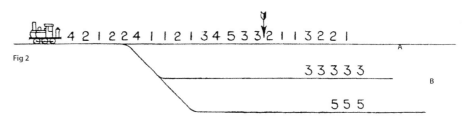
Fig 2

FIG. 2 We continue to sort out the '3's and '5's; we now cut off where shown by the arrow. This gives the engine a load of 15 wagons, which includes the only other '5' there is to come, and all the '4's.

We bear in mind that when the last '5' has been shunted into siding B, the '4's may be placed against them; and similarly, when all the '3's have been shunted into siding A, the '2's may be placed against them.

Note there is a single '3' among the wagons left on the train road, and at first sight it may appear that this wagon must be placed against its fellows in siding A before the '2's can be shunted into that siding. But this is not so, because when the wagons on the engine have been shunted off, the whole of the '4's will have been sorted out, and will stand 'open'; and therefore, when the last portion of the train comes to be shunted, this wagon '3' will be in its right position if it is placed against the '4's. This will become clear later; at the present moment the wagons on the engine are as in Fig. 3.

Fig 3

FIG. 3 After shunting off the two '3's, we come to the last of the '5's, and next to it is a '4'. Now, as the '4's have finally to stand against the '5's, we shall not separate these two wagons, but shunt them off together. We place the next 3 into siding A, and as this is the last of the '3's on the engine, we shall place against it all the '2's that follow, and shall place the '4's, of course, into siding B. We make, in all, 11 shunts in disposing of this batch of wagons, and the position is then as given in Fig. 4.

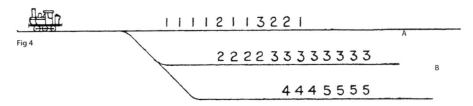
Fig 4

FIG. 4 We now require siding room for sorting out the last portion of the train. Therefore, we shall clear siding B by transferring the '5's and '4's into their final position on the train road. We must first pick up the wagons on the train road, back them against those in B, draw all over the points and set back on to the train road. We detach the '4's and '5's, and the situation then is as in Fig. 5.

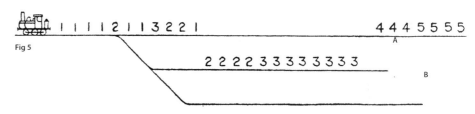
Fig 5

FIG. 5 Next, we shunt '1' into B, two '2's against their fellows in A, the '3' against the '4s' standing open on the train road, and then the two '1's against their fellow wagon we have just placed into B.

Left on the engine now is four '1's and a '2'. As this is our last '2', we shall not separate it from the '1's, but attach these wagons to those in siding A, and draw out all from that siding, to be placed into their final position. This gives us the position shown in Fig. 6.

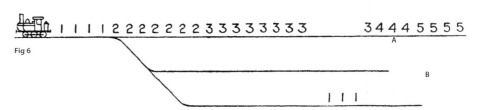
Fig 6

FIG. 6 Finally, we pick up the three '1's from siding B, and place them against their fellows on the train.

The marshalling performance just described was on well-defined lines, and would pass for a sample of quite good work; but rarely, if ever, is any general plan sufficiently applicable to obtain the best results throughout particular operations. It is just here that the shunter's observation, foresight and skill enable him to supplement such a plan with exceptional manoeuvres here and there that are peculiarly suitable to the task of the moment. This is the subject of our next example.

OPPOSITE The connection between Gresford Colliery sidings and the old GWR line is shown in this picture, taken in 1965. Note the fence that marked the division between the railway company lines and the private siding and the gate accross the line. *P. J. Garland Collection*

Shunting Example 5

The complexities of the work in a marshalling yard were always changing; they were never twice the same; the composition of every train was different; every shunting performance presented features of its own, and it was only by having due regard to these that the most appropriate movements could be decided upon. From this point of view we examine again the marshalling operation that has been worked out in different ways in the preceding examples. We have a train of 30 thoroughly 'mixed' wagons for five destinations and only two sidings, each with room for not more than 12 wagons in which to handle them. The train is shown in Fig. 1.

FIG. 1 It will be seen that the wagons are in ones and twos throughout, but here and there are standing together two or three for successive destinations (viz 2-3, 2-2-3, 3-3-4, 3-4, 4-5), and bear in mind that if we can contrive to keep some of them together we shall save the work of uncoupling, separately shunting, and recoupling them. The crux of the present situation is the shortage of working room, and therefore the sooner we can get some of the wagons shunted finally outside our narrow working limits, and thereby give ourselves more space for handling the others, the more we shall simplify the work. This means that the wagons that have finally to go to the rear of the marshalled train (the '5's) should be got into that position as early as practicable.

FIG. 2 With the '5's soon to be placed out of the way, the 'foundation' wagons for one siding should be '4's, and the '3's placed against them; on the principle of alternate destinations for different sidings, the other siding should take the '2's.

Meanwhile, throughout the movements, the '1's should be separated from the others by being worked to next the engine. At the first cut-off from the train, we take away three wagons (4-2-3). By making the separation here, the first '1' on the train will later come next to the engine. Moreover, the wagons taken away will provide the 'foundations' for both sidings, for the '3' may rightly stand behind the '2', because that will be its final position on the train, and we save shunting by treating these two wagons as a single unit. We shunt these into siding A and the '4' into siding B. The engine now returns light to the train. Fig. 2 shows the present position and the next cut-off. *

Again we divide the wagons immediately in front of '1's, so that at the next cut-off we shall bring three '1's together. Again we avoid separating companion wagons by shunting off 3-3-4 together into B, and likewise 5-5-2-2 into A. We retain '1' on the engine and the position is as in Fig. 3.

FIG. 3 We are now building up the '5's and '3's. That four wagons stand behind the '5's in A is to the good, as they are out of the way of our immediate aim. We shunt the two '3's into B, the '5' into A, and return to the train with 1-1-1 on the engine. The position now is as in Fig. 4.

FIG. 4 Standing 'open' in the sidings are '3' and '5'. It will be seen that we can build up on these by cutting off where shown by the arrow. After putting off the two '3's, the next wagon is the last of the '5's and, as this will be the front of the '5's on the marshalled train, we shall leave its companion ('4') coupled to it.

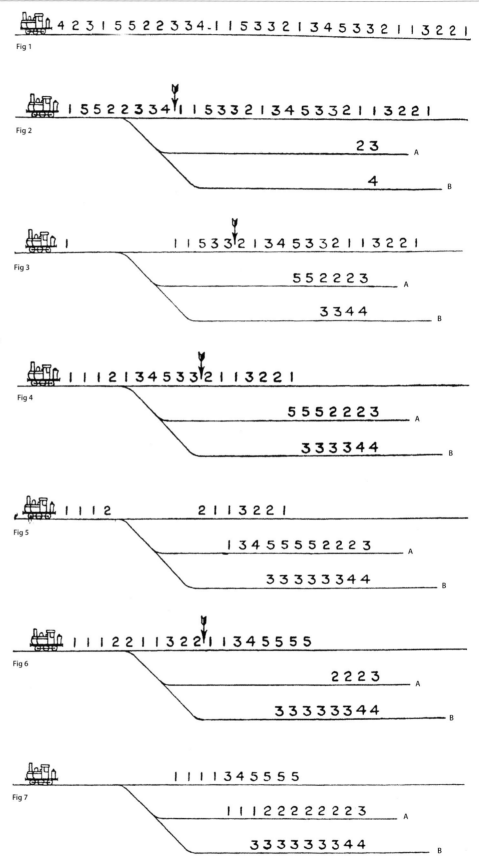

Fig 1

Fig 2

Fig 3

Fig 4

Fig 5

Fig 6

Fig 7

Shunting Example 6

At this point we are able to make a useful manoeuvre. Its advantage will be best understood by reviewing the movements after they have been completed. Meanwhile, the reader should take note of the wagons concerned, and observe the results attained during the procedure. In the process of operations we shall contrive, without an extra shunt, to bring together:

(a) the '2' on the engine and the '2' now standing open on the train;

(b) the '1' between the '2' and '3' on the engine and the '1' at the end of the train;

(c) the remaining '3' on the engine and its fellows in siding B.

In putting into A the wagons 4-5 (as described above), we do not uncouple them from the others, but leave with them the adjoining 1-3, cutting off behind the 2, giving the position shown in Fig. 5.

FIG. 5 We shall now clear the train road in order to place the '5's and one '4' into their final position. In picking up the last portion of the train, we bring together the two '2's (a) above. We draw forward all the wagons and back them into siding A (which brings together the two '1's [b] above). Then we bring out the '5's, and place them (and the 4) on to the train road. This gives the position shown in Fig. 6.

FIG. 6 For the moment we also leave the wagons 1-1-3 on the train road, so that those now standing 'open' on the respective roads are '1', '2' and '3'. We shunt off the wagons accordingly, until we come to the last 2-2, and when placing these into A we let the three '1's on the engine go with them. We now have the position shown in Fig. 7.

FIG. 7 All that remains to be done is to take five wagons from the train road (1-1-1-3). With these on the engine, pick up all from B; bringing together the two '3's (c) above, put these on the train road and then, with the four '1's on the engine, pick up all the wagons in A and place them against the others.

I believe that Hadley made a mistake and at this point he did not quote the correct numbers. His first shunt of three wagons – 3, 3, 4 – should be either 5, 2, 2, 3, 3, 4 or one of the 3s if his first cut is a 2. If we accept this is an error in his published work then the remainder of his example makes sense. As this is the only published work that explains how shunting was carried out, for historical reasons his original text has been retained and this footnote added.

Suppose you have to put away a train that has arrived with a thoroughly 'mixed' load of 30 wagons for five different destinations, and you are going to use a separate siding for each destination. Such a train is shown below, and the figures indicate the sidings into which the wagons are to be shunted.

FIG. 1 Although this is a usual and straightforward job, there is no generally established way of going about it. Every one of 20 shunters would do it differently, and with widely varying expenditures of time and labour.

The man habituated to 'long' shunting would be apt to draw all the 30 wagons over the points, and then to shunt them off in ones and twos just as they came to him. This is the worst possible method; it would occupy the yard more than twice as long as was necessary, and give the engine more than double the work that the job actually demanded.

Of the men who would recognise the disadvantages of beginning the shunting with so large a number of wagons on the engine, many would proceed at once to divide the train at about the middle, so as to dispose of it in two portions. Thus, the first portion would be as shown.

FIG. 2 This method would be an improvement upon the one first described, but still it would be an extravagance in terms of time, labour and engine power.

Observe that the third wagon to be shunted is for No 5 siding, and next come two wagons for siding No 1. There would be a considerable distance between the points for these two sidings and, when the wagon for No 5 was shunted off, the engine and the string of 13 wagons still attached to it would not be likely to be ahead of the points for No 1, so as to enable the points for No 1 to be 'saved'; and therefore the engine would

have to be reversed and the wagons drawn ahead. It will be seen that a No 1 follows a No 5 at two places in the first portion of the train.

A shunter who uses his wits to do the work in the quickest and lightest manner will contrive to avoid going to the more distant sidings more than once if he can, and will divide the train at such places as will enable him to shunt first into the nearer sidings. We will describe this procedure in detail.

The first division of the train is shown below. Before the wagons are uncoupled, the whole train is drawn up, so that the engine will not have to run back so far to pick up the second portion.

FIG. 3 The shunter tells the driver that he has cut off 13 wagons and instructs him to draw well over the points for the wagons to be shunted off in ones and twos, and the points to be 'saved'. He shunts into their sidings the wagons 1-1, 4, 3-3 and 2-2. Next come 5-5, but instead of placing these into No 5 siding, he shunts them back on to the second portion of the train. Then he shunts into their sidings the wagons '1', '3', '2' and, keeping the last wagon ('4') on the engine, returns to the train and couples up. His next division of the train is shown below.

FIG. 4 The next procedure is to shunt off, in turn, the wagons 3, 1, 2, 3-3, keep the rest of the wagons (4, 5-5-5) on the engine and back on to the train, which is then formed thus:

FIG. 5 It will be seen that next to the engine are six wagons, all there are for the more distant sidings, Nos 4 and 5. These six wagons are then taken away and shunted into their sidings, and the engine returns light for the final portion of the train, which consists of wagons for only the nearer sidings, Nos 1, 2 and 3.

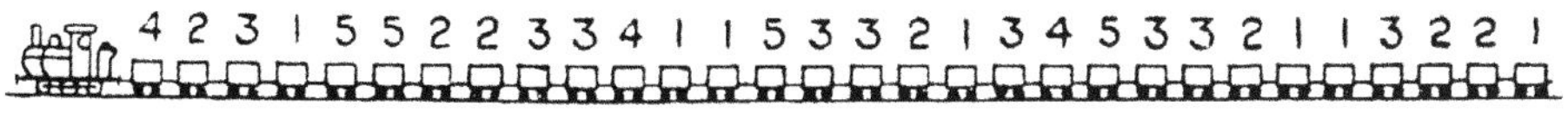

4 2 3 1 5 5 2 2 3 3 4 1 1 5 3 3 2 1 3 4 5 3 3 2 1 1 3 2 2 1

Fig 1

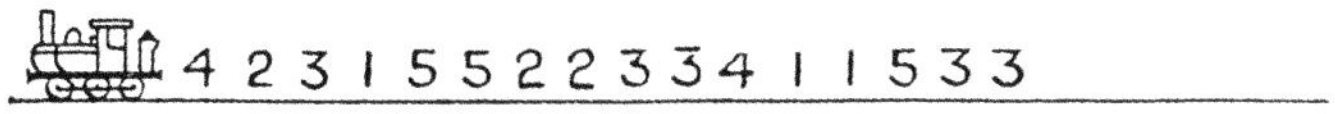

4 2 3 1 5 5 2 2 3 3 4 1 1 5 3 3

Fig 2

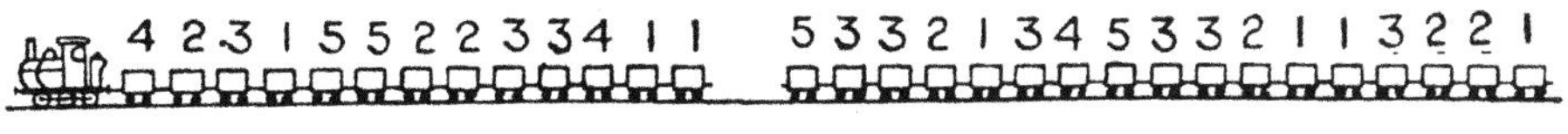

4 2 3 1 5 5 2 2 3 3 4 1 1   5 3 3 2 1 3 4 5 3 3 2 1 1 3 2 2 1

Fig 3

4 5 5 5 3 3 2 1 3 4 5 3 3 2 1 1 3 2 2 1

Fig 4

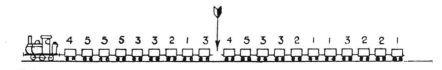

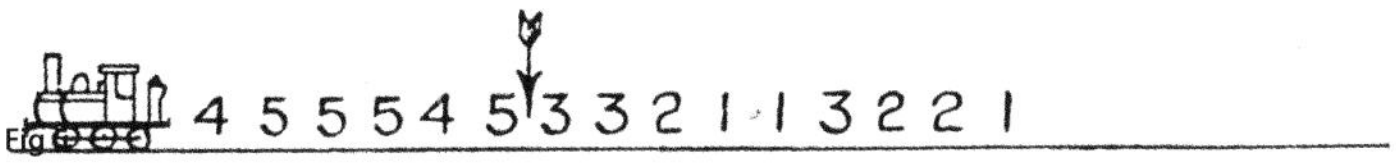

4 5 5 5 4 5 3 3 2 1 1 3 2 2 1

Fig 5

LEFT The marshalling yard at Perth was rather empty when this undated picture was taken; the official photographer was in a lighting tower, which enables the layout of the sidings to be seen. Note how most sidings are in groups of six, made up of two smaller groups of three. In the lower left-hand side, the short length of track connects the first group of three sidings with the second group. This was a 'slip road', very useful if you were shunting and needed to run round wagons.
British Railways

5 Marshalling locomotives

Many readers may be surprised to know that locomotives were shunted, although the term more commonly used was 'marshalled'. When visiting model railway exhibitions, it soon becomes clear that many modellers tend to use their engine sheds more like dumping grounds for engines not in use. And so, while this book is largely devoted to shunting rolling stock, we should not overlook shunting at engine sheds. Apart from locomotives themselves, which we will deal with later, most of the wagon shunting at a locomotive shed was of locomotive coal wagons – both loaded and empty. These arrived at regular intervals and could be no more than a single wagonload for a shed, with only one or two locomotives or complete trainloads for depots with a large allocation.

Depending upon the layout of the shed, there may have been a form of mechanical coaling plant. In some, loaded coal wagons were raised up and the contents tipped into the bunker before being transferred to the locomotive's tender on tank engines, while others were coaling stages where wagons were propelled up an incline so that the coal could be unloaded into tubs before being tipped into bunkers or tenders. There were numerous variations of mechanical equipment and hand coaling methods, but all required the loaded coal wagons to be

shunted to where the coal was unloaded and the empty wagons removed.

In addition to coal traffic, there were wagons and vans that delivered stores and removed worn parts – for example, brake blocks that had been taken off an engine and empty wagons that, when loaded, carried away the ash and clinker removed from the locomotives' fire grates, ashpans and smokeboxes. Sand was also a requirement – very small sheds received dried sand, but most sheds had their own sand-drying ovens; this traffic – loads of wet

sand in and empties out – required shunting too. All these vehicles were shunted as required at locomotive sheds.

At large depots there would probably be a shed pilot to carry out this work and, when required, to move dead engines – i.e. engines not in steam and therefore not moving under their own power. Many locomotive depots were crammed full on a Sunday night with engines that would start to leave the shed from the early hours of Monday morning. As I recall from personal experience, Saltley shed had three large roundhouses; after

This 10 March 1910 interior view of Derby No 4 roundhouse shows it was possible to build roundhouses adjacent to each other; locomotives in the far roundhouse were moved from the stall road onto the turntable and then run over the second turntable out of the shed. This was a better arrangement than a straight shed, reducing the amount of shunting (or marshalling) required and ensuring locomotives were where they should be for their next turn of duty.

completing their Saturday or Sunday work, many locomotives were placed in the shed yard. They were still in steam and were looked after by the steam raiser, until a set of enginemen took charge of them. From midnight on Sunday and to a lesser degree into the week, sets of men would shunt these engines around. Some were engaged in preparing engines, so that they were ready when the men who were to take them off-shed booked on, but at least one set would be engaged in simply shunting the locomotives about to ensure that an engine was not at the end of a siding or blocked in by other locomotives when it was required.

On model railways that have engine sheds and work to an operational sequence, there are opportunities for shunting locomotives. For example, on a small shed, if the last engine to come on-shed is one of the first to leave the following day, it does not matter if it is blocking the exit of another engine; but if the last in is not the first out, then some degree of shunting has to take place (as the

accompanying photographs and diagram should make clear).

Generally, modellers base their own versions on smaller engine sheds, with an allocation of ten or less locomotives, but I have seen models where the allocation is much greater. Whatever the size, it is most important to get the on-shed sequence right; while it may not be shunting in the generally accepted sense, the marshalling of engines is still a form of it. Generally, across the British railway system it was a case of: 1) fill the tank; 2) take on coal; 3) clean or drop the fire, then empty the ashpan and smokebox

ABOVE This 1930s view of the old LNWR engine shed at Edge Hill illustrates how crowded engine sheds could be at times. Two locomotives are 'blowing off', ready to depart, while the fireman of No 16486 has a long clinker shovel which suggests the engine is being prepared, but he is not satisfied with the condition of the 'fire in the box' – to use an engineman's words. This picture makes the point that engines had to be marshalled so that those required for duty were not stuck inside the shed, with others blocking their exit.

(although a self-cleaning smokebox only received attention if the locomotive was to have the boiler washed out); 4) turn if required; 5) stable over an inspection pit.

When arriving on-shed, 3) might precede 2), and 4) could be the first part of the process. At sheds where there was insufficient room, engines were placed on sidings without inspection pits. Before they could be prepared, they had to be moved (shunted) to stand on an inspection pit road so that the driver could oil and inspect the entire engine. (I included a chapter on engine sheds in *Railway Operation for the Modeller*, which readers may find helpful.)

LEFT This is the small locomotive shed at Middleton Top on the Cromford and High Peak line, where one or sometimes two locomotives were stationed, seen on 5 June 1950. Other than simple coaling facilities and water, the shed was little more than a signing-on point for the enginemen stationed there. Shunting here would be minimal. *T. J. Edgington*

ABOVE The movement of loaded locomotive coal wagons required the attention of a shunting engine; at large sheds there may have been a dedicated shed pilot, but at smaller sheds the work was probably undertaken by locomotives that had arrived at the end of a turn of duty. This picture of a coaling stage at Burton on Trent in 1946 shows a number of wagons waiting to be unloaded. As this was done, the empty wagons would be pushed through until the line to the buffer stop was full, then the empties were shunted to the side and full wagons returned to the stage. At some stages there was an incline at both sides that enabled loaded wagons to be fed in from one end and empty wagons to be taken from the other. However, the majority were built like the example shown here.

LEFT TOP In this early 1950s picture, taken at Saltley on a Sunday afternoon, we can see the need to shunt engines to allow others to be prepared. The three roundhouses would probably be full and engines that could not be kept under cover were standing in the shed yard. From about midnight onwards, sets of men would begin to prepare engines. When they were ready the locomotives stood in the yard, usually on sidings to the left of the coal tower, waiting for the crews to take over. By Monday morning, many of the engines would have left the shed but incoming locomotives from trains that had terminated in the area would start to arrive. To cope with this, there was a least one set of men whose work was shunting engines to enable others to be released.

LEFT BOTTOM One variation of the roundhouse – which had the turntable in the centre of the shed – was to build the outside wall on a curve and arrange the exit lines to run onto a turntable that was outside the shed. It can be seen in this picture of the shed at Eastbourne on the old London, Brighton and South Coast Railway. In many respects this is an ideal layout for modellers, provided such an arrangement can be justified.
NRM BURTT 134

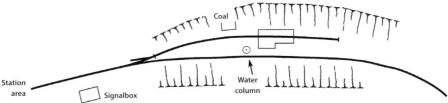

ABOVE This drawing of a single-road shed is based upon the GWR depot at Pontrilas. If used as the basis of a design by a modeller for his layout, it would probably hold one or two locomotives. If it was two locomotives, the engine roster would probably ensure the last engine in was the first out. If it was three engines, then some shunting would almost certainly be required to make sure the engine at the rear of the shed was the last one to leave in the morning.

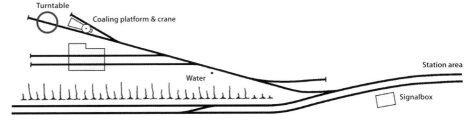

ABOVE This shed layout is based upon Leominster and shows a two-road shed with a water crane, coaling platform and turntable. A shed of this type would probably hold four to six locomotives, with engines required to turn running along one side of the coaling platform while those that did not need to turn would be coaled on the other side. With two shed roads, space to place an engine on the coal stage road (without fouling the shed road) and a short siding near the running lines, the locomotives could be marshalled to ensure the first out was not at the back of the shed when required.

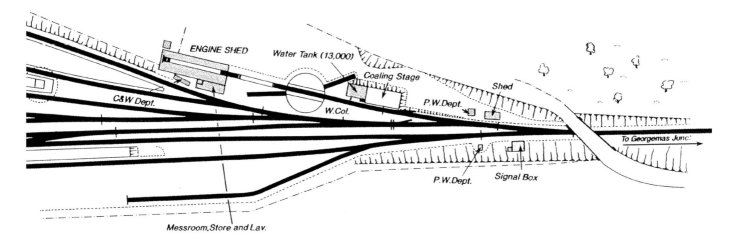

BELOW In many respects, Thurso is an ideal prototype for modellers to use when designing their imaginary layouts. There is a station, small goods yard and engine shed close to each other in this April 1952 picture, showing a 4-4-0 No 54398 engaged in shunting duties, probably making up a train that will shortly depart towards Georgemas Junction. *P. B. Whitehouse*

ABOVE Modellers could use this sketch of Thurso as the basis for a simple terminus. Although not unique, there were not many engine sheds in the UK where access was over a turntable. Note the two short sidings off the table that could be used when marshalling, to ensure that an engine at the back of the shed was not blocked in when it was required.

RIGHT When private companies used their own locomotives to shunt and marshal inwards and outwards traffic, small engine sheds were required. This picture was taken *c*1960 at Walkden colliery, Manchester and shows the small two-road engine shed with three locomotives. *P. B. Whitehouse*

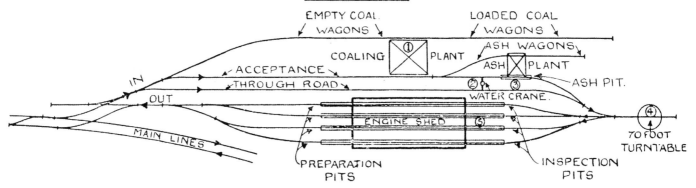

DIAGRAM OF
MOTIVE POWER DEPOT,
SHEWING SEQUENCE OF DISPOSAL
OPERATIONS.

During the 1930s, the need to modernise shed layouts and the availability of low-interest government loans saw many improvements made to shed layouts. This diagram, taken from the *LMS Magazine*, shows an ideal layout for a shed. The example given is a four-road through shed but the same sequence would apply to both a larger or smaller version. Many layouts led to delays while coaling, for example – until the engine in front has been coaled, those behind had to wait to take their turn at the stage. The key was to ensure a progressive sequence of movements from the time the engine arrived on shed until it reached the point where it was to be stabled, or until it left the shed yard again for traffic working. The diagram illustrates an ideal running shed yard layout with arrows showing the course taken by engines and the sequence of five movements to complete the whole process of disposal:

1/ 2) Coaling/Watering: some locations allow these to be carried out simultaneously;

3) Cleaning or lifting fire and emptying the ashpan;

4) Turning when required;

5) Stabling in shed.

Note the arrangement of the connection to the running lines – the arrivals and departures have separate lines. The loaded coal wagons are kept at the buffer stop end of the siding and drawn towards the coaling plant as required, thereby allowing empties to be removed easily without having to shunt away loaded coal wagons if the loads were kept at the arrival end of the siding. Both the acceptance and through road allow engines to run either way and so, depending upon their next scheduled duty, engines can be stabled at either end of the shed.

6 Types of engines employed

This final chapter considers some of the locomotive types that were used for shunting purposes. Many years ago, I recall being told by my driver that a good shunting engine would accelerate quickly and stop smartly. What he did not say was that engines engaged, to a lesser or greater degree, in shunting covered a wide range: from small 0-4-0 tank engines to large passenger tender engines, the former usually employed at sidings where the curves were sharp, the latter to shunt empty coaching stock into another platform or carriage siding as part of their diagrammed work.

The most common wheel arrangement for locomotives built for shunting purposes was the 0-6-0T, with 0-6-0 tender engines in second place as far as locomotives used for shunting were concerned. Regardless of wheel arrangement, the most important feature for a shunting engine was the method of reversing. A lever reverser was far better than a screw reverser; it could be thrown over very quickly, whereas with a screw reverser the driver had to make a number of turns before he could open the regulator and begin to move. Which brings us to the question of shunting on model railways.

When propelling wagons over a hump, the shunting engine moved slowly and may have taken the entire train over the hump without stopping, but when shunting on the flat it was different. The train was drawn back along the shunting line and then, when signalled by the shunter, the driver would try to accelerate

quickly and stop smartly, leaving the wagons that had been uncoupled to roll forward into the siding. The locomotive's movements were forward/stop, forward/stop and so on. While it was possible on the full-size railway to shunt an entire train without reversing the shunting engine, a little reversing was usually the case. This was in order to draw the rest of the train back along the shunting line to allow a sufficient length of siding for the forward/stop movements to continue. (These are covered in detail in Chapter 4.) With a model, neither method is easy; getting model wagons on a smaller scale to roll like the prototype is virtually impossible. Model railway shunting is therefore more akin to placing wagons on sidings.

This was done to some degree with goods stock on the prototype, but it was the correct method with coaches. The coach was pushed forward until the buffers touched the vehicle in front, and then it was either coupled to that

vehicle or else the brakes were applied before it was uncoupled from the engine.

Although shunting was carried out by steam engines until the end of the steam era, it became clear the use of a diesel-shunting engine was far more cost-effective. In Great Britain, the LMS led the way in the development of diesel-shunting engines, but by the time of nationalisation the number available was small compared with the number of steam locomotives used for this work. Modellers of the pre-1968 period should be aware of this when selecting shunting units to work on their layouts. Unless it was to travel over running lines, a diesel-shunting engine required only a driver and was available for the entire week – whereas a steam engine required a driver and firemen, stores and servicing.

Two examples taken from a 1955 timetable should suffice to make this point. Burton on Trent Trip 113 was described as the Hawkins

LEFT Among the most successful classes of steam locomotives to be employed for shunting and local freight working were the various GWR 0-6-PTs engines, with some remaining in British Railways service until the end of steam. This 7 July 1921 view was taken at Lostwithiel and shows one of the earlier locomotives, No 1746, engaged in shunting.

RIGHT When this picture was taken on 17 June 1968, the end of steam power on British Railways was only a few weeks away. It shows a Class 5MT No 44802 carrying Class K stopping freight train headcode, shunting at Bolton. This is a good example of a trip working that detached and attached traffic during the course of its diagrammed work. *R. W. Courtney*

Lane shunting engine and was worked by a Class 3F 0-6-0T. It was required to shunt from 6.15am Monday until 3am on Sunday, working trips between Hawkins Lane Yard, Burton Goods and Old Dixie. It went to Burton shed at 1am each day from Tuesday to Saturday for servicing and to take on coal, clean the fire, empty the ashpan and smokebox, meaning it was probably not available for work for about two hours each day. On the other hand, a diesel engine did not require returning to shed. An example of this can be seen with Saltley Shunting Engine No 2, Lawley Street Nos 1 & 2 Goods Sheds. The locomotive left Saltley Shed at 5.55am Monday and was available to shunt from 6am until 10pm Sunday, whereupon it returned to Saltley shed. During the early hours of Monday, the same locomotive could be prepared to depart from the shed at 5.55am in order to start another week's work.

As we have seen, shunting was carried out in a wide variety of locations ranging from large marshalling yards, passenger and goods stations to small roadside stations and private sidings. When we consider this, it soon

becomes clear that the 0-6-0T was not always suitable for all tasks and the different names given to various shunting turns are helpful when defining their work. It is also worth noting that, while many shunting engines were not equipped with automatic brakes, whether vacuum or Westinghouse, one or both was essential if the locomotive was to shunt coaching and/or fitted freight stock.

To begin with the station pilot, the duty of this locomotive was to shunt coaching stock – both passenger and non-passenger carrying vehicles – at those major stations where a station pilot was required. However, while a 0-6-0T was often suitable for this work, there were locations where a passenger tender engine was required. (An example of this is given at page 45 in Chapter 3.)

The final point to be made is that, although the mechanics of an engine shunting wagons have been described, when shunting coaching stock the opposite technique was required. Attaching coaches to a train standing in a station had to be approached very carefully indeed; as one of my drivers told me when I was allowed to drive one day, 'You approach so carefully that you should be able to hold an egg between the buffers and not break it!' I took the point.

In addition to the work carried out by dedicated shunting engines, a lot of goods shunting was performed by trip workings. As I have mentioned previously, the names and descriptions used by one company were not always used by another. We therefore need a flexible approach when viewing railway practice employed by British companies during the steam era.

On the LNWR *c*1920, their local trip workings were identified by a board carried on the right-hand lamp socket that displayed the trip number, described in the working timetable as the 'target number'. In a copy of a 1927 WTT (Working Time Table), the same rules applied on what had been the Furness Railway, by then part of the LMS Western Division, where local trip and shunting engines

LEFT Another very successful class of shunting engines, the Midland 0-6-0Ts, formed the basis of the standard LMS class commonly referred to as 'Jinties'. This undated British Railways period picture shows No 47223 shunting at Maiden Lane, where the overbridge carried the North London line over the old LNWR line.

LEFT This class of North Eastern Railway locomotives dated from 1875. From 1904 the company began to dispose of them, this particular locomotive (No 11) sold in 1911 to Backworth colliery where it remained in service until 1944. It was not unusual for the mainline railway companies to sell locomotives for industrial use on private railways.

RIGHT Sometimes passenger engines were used to work goods trains and undertake shunting duties, as seen in this and some of the following pictures. This is an ex-Midland Railway 0-4-4T No 58071, photographed at Ashchurch on 6 September 1952. The locomotive is an ex-London district, condenser-fitted engine that still retains the tall brackets for the destination boards used to identify some trains in that area.

BELOW Industrial railways were often found in idyllic surroundings, which will appeal to many modellers. This picture was taken on 1 June 1967 and shows an Andrew Barclay 0-4-0ST shunting wagons to make up the Long Meg to Widnes anhydrites train; the old Midland mainline is just visible through the branches at the top of the picture. *Paul Cotterell*

were also numbered and carried on a target board. Similar numbered targets also existed elsewhere both before and after the grouping. During the early BR period, a Kilmarnock control area WTT included 'out of area trains' – my first encounter with this term. They were local workings to destinations outside the control area that also carried a target board. This timetable included all trip and shunting turns that were individually numbered and stated that the locomotive should carry a target board. The point to be made was that their trip or target numbers identified local freight workings within any particular area in the various timetables. A similar approach applied to shunting turns in various sidings, with these locomotives also referred to as 'yard pilots'. However, photographic evidence suggests the use of target boards was far from universal, particularly during the British Railways period. It was probably more prevalent when more than one engine was shunting at the same time in the same area and was used to assist railwaymen in identifying the locomotives.

In addition to the work carried out by dedicated shunting engines, shunting was performed during trip workings – which brings me to the need to explain what these actually were. Although I have never seen a description of this work in print, in my view it is best described as local non-passenger work within a given operating area. The various trips would be numbered generally from one upwards, with a similar approach applied in adjacent areas sometimes described as an operating superintendent's district. The work would range from dedicated shunting turns or engines rostered to banking duties, as well as trains

moving wagons, either loaded or empty, from A to B. In the major cities and towns, where there could be more than one marshalling yard and several goods stations, one or more daily trip workings would be employed transferring wagons from one yard to another. 'Trippers', as they were sometimes called, would also carry out transfers between two railway companies or, after 1948, two regions of British Railways. The movement of wagons to collect from sidings could entail a colliery, gas or electric power station, or any other industrial company with private sidings or a canal wharf; the trip working could also take place between goods yards that formed part of a passenger station. The list is almost endless.

The usual modellers' term is 'pickup goods', which was also used to describe trains that delivered to or collected wagons from stations along a line, whether it be a country branch or a section of main line. As mentioned previously, the same names and descriptions for similar work were not always used by all railway companies, so a flexible approach is required when studying past practice. (I tend to use terms that applied to the LMS companies, which may not be universal across the British railway system.)

In this chapter, I have included a variety of pictures to show shunting engines and trip workings that might involve varying degrees of shunting. The line between a trip working and what many enthusiasts call a 'pickup freight' is rather fine – but the subject has already been covered in *Freight Train Operation for the Railway Modeller.*

LEFT This picture was probably taken pre-1914. It shows an LNWR 'Watford' class 0-6-2T engaged in shunting empty covered goods wagons. The point to note is that the doors of two vehicles are open; later regulations stated they should be closed before the vehicles were moved.

ABOVE Station pilots could be tender or tank engines, old or modern designs, but they had to be fitted with an automatic brake and (usually) carriage-warming equipment during the carriage-warming season. Here we see an old LNWR Special Tank No 7400 on station pilot duty.

RIGHT An ex-Caledonian Railway 0-4-4T No 15232 is shown engaged in shunting. It can be assumed that this is a local trip working and the man standing by the engine with the shunting pole is the guard of the train. It was common practice at small stations for the guard to be in charge and for him to undertake this work, but at some locations a porter/shunter would assist him. *A. G. Ellis*

LEFT ABOVE The Highland Railway used their 4-4-0s for both passenger and goods workings, which continued after 1923 when the company became part of the LMS. In this 20 June 1927 picture we see No 14279 engaged in shunting at Kyle of Lochalsh. The goods sidings were adjacent to the passenger station and, after arriving with the passenger train, the coaches are at the platform; the locomotive was rostered to shunt the yard. *H. C. Casserley*

LEFT BELOW Passing Gresty Lane is ex-LMS 0-6-0T No 47494 bringing stock into Crewe station. The leading vehicle is a covered goods van equipped with automatic vacuum brake followed by a bogie parcels van, but we cannot see the rest of the train. As one of several pilots its target number is carried on a 'target board' – in this case white on black, mounted between the locomotive headlamps. *J. S. Hancock*

RIGHT This shows ex-LNWR 4-4-0 No 25277 shunting a Cattle Fair Special at Tal-y-cafn on the Conway Valley branch in 1942. The station was on a single line with a passing loop and the sidings could only be entered via a point controlled by a ground frame, opposite the signal on the right of this picture. At times it was necessary to shunt with vehicles, in this case the brakevan, 'on the engine'. *Mile Post 92½*

ABOVE LMS Class 4Fs were frequently employed on local trip work, as confirmed by the headlamp code on display. Photographed at Grimesthorpe on 27 August 1939, this shows No 4128 with the driver looking back, the shunter with the pole looking at the photographer and another man just visible at the doorway of the 10T Ballast brakevan, behind the tender.

RIGHT Pannier tanks of various types were often employed for station pilot duties on the Western Region, but not always – as this picture of 2-6-2T No 5523 at Bristol Temple Meads shows. The locomotive is coupled to a Siphon G when standing on one of the centre roads, prior to attaching the vehicle to a passenger train that will arrive in due course. *Steve Banks Collection*

LEFT ABOVE This mid-1950s view taken at Grantham shows ex-GNR 'C12' class 4-4-2 No 67397 at the head of secondary coaching stock. Station pilots carried their headcode, one lamp over each buffer, at both ends of the locomotive; when lit, each end would display a white and red light. The use of lamps at both ends can be clearly seen in this picture. *Neville Stead Collection*

LEFT BELOW Shunting engines in goods yards on the GWR, or the post-1948 Western Region, were almost always coupled to a shunter's truck. This view, taken at Weymouth on 23 June 1956, shows ex-GWR 0-6-0PT No 9620 (a yard pilot) coupled to a shunter's truck. Because the locomotive and shunter's truck were considered a single operational unit, the locomotive headlamps are carried on the front of the engine and the rear of the truck. *Steve Banks Collection*

RIGHT When photographed at Edge Hill on 17 June 1948, LNWR Coal Tank No 7751 was carrying mineral train headlamp code. This may have been correct or maybe it was just 'slack working', as some firemen were not too particular about the headlamp code for light engines or stopping freight trains. (The headlamp was to be on the centre lamp holder for light engines and on the left hand – facing forward – for stopping freight trains.) This appears to be a local trip working and the man with the shunting pole is the guard. The locomotive is fitted with a vacuum-controlled regulator; note the two vacuum pipes at the front of the engine, for use when operating passenger stock during the working of motor trains. *M. J. Robertson Collection*

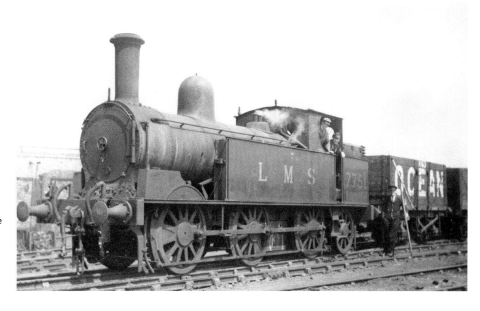

LEFT Photographed at Elmers End on 22 September 1958, this shows ex SR 'C' class 0 6 0 No 31719 blowing off steam while shunting in the station goods yard. Judging by the position of the fireman, they have stopped to have their 'snap'. *Peter Tatlow*

RIGHT This picture, taken at Fenchurch Street on the Great Eastern Railway on 21 August 1911, illustrates a locomotive turntable. Locomotives could gain access to the table from the running line, although why there were two water columns is far from clear. Some engine diagrams allowed tender-first return working, but others required the engine to be turned and this was not always carried out at locomotive depots. This appears to be a locomotive servicing point where engines can be turned and water taken. There is an inspection pit, seen between the two columns, and on the left we can see a pit where fires can be cleaned and the ashpans raked out. Note the few wagons that are standing on the various sidings, showing how it was not always necessary to have everything neat and tidy. *NRM GE 895*

LEFT CENTRE Double-headed engines engaged on shunting duties were rather unusual, but here we can see a pair of 2-6-2Ts Nos 82015 and 41293 at Bevois Park, Southampton, with a transfer working from the docks. *Peter Tatlow*

RIGHT BELOW Photographed at Inverness in 1930, we see 0-4-0ST No 16040 engaged in shunting duties. Short wheelbase locomotives were built for shunting at locations where the curves were too sharp for longer wheelbase engines; docks, collieries and industrial works are good examples of where they would be found. *J. A. G. H. Coltas*

LEFT BELOW This picture, taken at Beauchief in April 1895, confirms that, apart from the size of the engines and stock, nothing much changed during the last 80 or so years of the steam railway in the United Kingdom – at least as far as trip working was concerned. Here we see a single-frame Midland Railway goods engine, later known as a '2F', engaged in shunting duties. The driver and fireman are on the engine and the guard and shunter are holding their shunting poles. It is not clear who the other person is – most likely a railway officer, or perhaps the stationmaster.

ABOVE LEFT Limited space means that many modellers have to build quite small stations which nonetheless include goods facilities; while some stations were passenger traffic only, they were in the minority. This picture, taken at Coughton in 1952, shows how shunting could be carried out at quite small locations. There was a single line through the station and a loop with a loading dock at the end of the platform (to the left of the picture). No signalbox was necessary; the station was in the block section and access to the siding was via two ground frames, one at each end of the loop. The tablet carried by the driver (to authorise access to the section) released the points. Not all passenger trains stopped and there was only one goods train per day in each direction that detached or attached wagons. A full description of the station may be found in *An Illustrated History of the Ashchurch to Barnt Green Line*.

ABOVE RIGHT A simpler arrangement than that of Coughton can be seen in the public sidings at Frankley on the Halesowen branch, September 1947. Some sources describe sidings of this type as 'mileage sidings' – where the traffic arrived to be loaded or unloaded by non-railway staff; the railway company charged mileage to bring the loaded wagon to the sidings or, if it was an empty wagon to be loaded, to take it to its destination. A similar arrangement applied to those at Coughton – a lever frame was unlocked by the train staff that was carried by the driver, to enable access to the siding. Sidings of this type can be incorporated in single-line model railways and provide opportunities for shunting to take place. (Frankley is described in *Midland Record 23*.)

RIGHT CENTRE With the iron ore tippler wagons dwarfing the engine, this 1950s view was taken on the old Great Central Railway at Charwelton. It shows a privately owned quarry locomotive shunting loaded wagons that will form a train to be worked away by a British Railways locomotive.

RIGHT This picture of old Midland Railway 0-4-0T No 1528 is another example of a short wheelbase locomotive employed on shunting duties; this picture was taken at Clay Cross works on 18 August 1934.
A. W. Croughton

ABOVE In this delightful setting we see an ex-Midland Railway 0-6-0 Class 2F No 58287, shunting at the old Furness station at Haverthwaite in the mid-1950s. The brakevan has been set aside while the required shunting moves take place; a tank wagon is coupled to the engine, but why the fireman is on the tender is not clear. *T. J. Edgington*

LEFT It was not unusual for steam locomotives to work across roads. The best example is probably Burton on Trent, where at one time there were more than 30 places where locomotives crossed roads in the town. This view was taken at Irwell Street crossing/Salford Goods station; the locomotive is an ex-L&Y 0-4-0T No 51237, seen on 10 November 1962. *T. J. Edgington*

BELOW LEFT The LMS built ten outside cylinder 0-6-0Ts (more powerful than the smaller 0-4-0Ts) for work at docks where the curves were sharp. This picture of No 47169 was taken at Ayr, where the locomotive was engaged in shunting duties.

LEFT TOP The old Great Northern Railway station at Stamford East was not very large; as we can see, its platform lines were used when shunting goods wagons. Photographed in August 1952, other pictures of 4-4-2T 'C12' class No 67361 taken on the same day show the engine on the line by the goods shed. This one has been selected because it shows, on the far left, a man moving the wagon with a wagon lever while another assists him by pushing.

LEFT CENTRE Some diagrams for trip working were allocated to large tender locomotives. This undated picture, taken at Stockport, shows a 'Super D' class No 9108 engaged in shunting duties while the shunter and his pole ride on the tender footsteps. *E. Kearns*

LEFT BELOW The problem of moving wagons within a goods shed is shown in this picture, taken at Workington on 27 August 1965. Fortunately, the tender could be coupled to the van just inside the shed, but if this had not been the case then reach wagons would have been required to enable the engine to be coupled to the vehicles and shunted away. *Paul Cotterell*

RIGHT I have included three pictures to show Alvechurch station; the first *(above)* is looking towards Redditch, showing the end of the blind siding and the small stage where the point lever was; the second *(centre)* is looking towards Barnt Green with wagons standing alongside the dock; the third *(below)* looks towards Redditch and the blind siding, with the connection between the main line and the siding. The top photograph was taken on 22 April 1958 by H. C. Casserley, the others by Joe Moss in August 1949.

My recollection of working this section of line in 1951/2 was that tow-roping had ceased and any traffic for Alvechurch from the south was taken forward to Washwood Heath, becoming part of a train for Redditch or beyond and detaching at Alvechurch. There were numerous stations in Great Britain where traffic could only be detached from or attached to trains travelling in one direction, so the wagons later came back to their destination as part of another train.

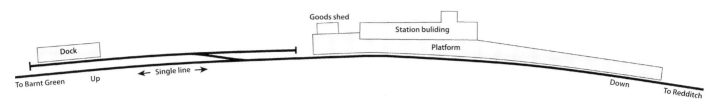

Goods shed

Station buliding

Dock

Platform

To Barnt Green Up ← Single line → Down To Redditch

ABOVE Although tow-roping was restricted in use on the prototype (during the early 1900s, the Board of Trade sought to reduce the number of places where it was permitted), the practice continued for many years. My experience of it was limited to Alvechurch, as described in *An Illustrated History of the Ashchurch to Barnt Green Line*, and this is a sketch of the Alvechurch track layout. It was a single line, with no passing loop or signalbox, and access to the siding was by a trailing point in the down direction.

A point lever was released by the token, which provided both the driver's authority to travel over the single line and entry to the siding. The station was on a falling gradient of 1-199 towards Redditch. Tow-roping was permitted to and from the dead-end siding; the siding alongside the dock held ten wagons while the short blind siding could hold about two. Tow-roping was carried out when an up train had wagons to detach.

Depending upon the wagons already there, it may have been necessary to move wagons from the dock to the blind siding close to the goods shed, but generally they would be drawn from the end of the train and put alongside the dock. The driver would stop clear of the points and the guard would screw down the brakevan's brake, pinning down the brakes at the end where the wagons were to be detached. He would then uncouple the wagons and the local shunter would attach the tow rope to them. The train engine would move over the points and take up the slack in the rope. The guard would unlock the points and the point lever would be reversed. The engine would start and the wagons would move into the siding, while the engine continued along the single line. When the wagons were in place, the tow rope would be removed, the points set and the engine put back onto the train, for it to be coupled and the brakes on the wagons and brakevan taken off. The guard would signal 'right away' and they were on their way.

Traffic for Alvechurch from the Barnt Green direction was detached in the normal way: train stopped clear of the points; brakes pinned down; wagons uncoupled from the train, before the same procedure with the points took place. It was possible to both attach and detach traffic when working a down train; if necessary, a down train could use a tow rope to move any wagons from the short siding, so that when they were clear of the points they could be coupled in the normal way. As can be seen, there were a number of permutations of what could be done both on the prototype and on a model.

LEFT This scene – a passenger train passing another locomotive shunting in adjacent sidings – can be found on many model railways, although modelling the scenery may be more difficult. Photographed at Quakers Yard (Low Level), we see a Merthyr to Pontypridd passenger train hauled by a GWR 0-6-0PT No. 9610 passing a former Taff Vale 0-6-2T No. 390 shunting in the yard. *Kidderminster Railway Museum*

RIGHT Here we see a Clayton Type 1 No D8590 shunting at Gilesgate goods station, Durham, on 5 August 1966. *I. S. Carr*

LEFT BELOW This rather interesting picture was taken at Llanthony sidings, on the Gloucester docks branch, on 2 January 1967 and shows a BR diesel shunter D2137 engaged in shunting. Note how the road-crossing gates are open for the road and closed against the railway; it was often the reverse, with long delays for road traffic. But if the sidings to the right of the picture are to be shunted then the gates will have to be opened for rail use and closed to road users, which may be why there is a man standing close to the gates. *Kidderminster Railway Museum*

RIGHT CENTRE LEFT Small Sentinel locomotives were built for certain shunting duties. They offer modellers the opportunity for something different on layouts where goods facilities or private sidings are sharply curved and space is minimal.

RIGHT CENTRE RIGHT Diesel shunting engines had many advantages over steam locomotives. From the 1930s, they began to take over the duties of steam shunters as steam power was phased out during the British Railway period up to 1968. This picture shows LMS No 7073 shunting at Carlisle in 1939. *S. H. Freeze*

BOTTOM LEFT During the final years of steam, the use of large locomotives to undertake trip and shunting duties became commonplace. While it is appropriate for modellers who seek to reproduce this era, it should be pointed out this practice did not really apply earlier. If a large engine that was normally used on express freight trains was rundown and waiting to go into the repair shops, then it could be rostered to work on local trips, but generally the railway companies tried to avoid what was seen as a waste of motive power. Here we see a Class 5MT No 45225 in the summer of 1965, photographed on what appears to be a trip working at Stalybridge. *David Birch*

RIGHT We conclude the book with something different. This picture was taken in 1958 and shows a Fordson Major with Muir-Hill modifications pulling 12 wagons. The advantage of using this form of motive power was that it did not run on rails, so it was very flexible in terms of what it could do. Quite how it could be incorporated into a model railway is perhaps another matter. *Ford Motor Co Ltd*

Glossary of terms

This is an expansion of the terms formerly listed in *Railway Operation for the Modeller*, beginning with those directly applicable to the subject of this book and concluding with some more general terms that readers may find helpful.

Some terms used in shunting and marshalling

Brakevan siding: A dedicated siding where brakevans were stabled prior to use on outward trains or held off inward trains when not required for traffic purposes. Some of these sidings were on steep gradients to allow brakevans to be moved by gravity and to roll to the rear of a train prior to departure.

Clear of: Not causing an obstruction.

Concentration yard: The modern alternative for marshalling yard. The term seems to have come into wider use about the same time as British Railways introduced TOPS (Total Operations Processing System).

Cripple siding: A siding where wagons labelled 'Not to Go' were placed awaiting repair; the wagon could be carrying a load. (Red label: 'Not to Go'; green label: 'For Repairs'.)

Departure sidings: Where trains were made up and placed prior to departure.

Derailers: Fulfilled the same function as a **trap point**.

Double shunting: The turning of some vehicles onto one line or siding and others onto another during a single propelling movement.

Dress the siding: An alternative to the expression **set**, meaning to arrange wagons on a siding for loading or unloading.

Exchange sidings: One or more sidings where traffic was exchanged between two or more different railway companies or operating divisions of the same company – or, alternatively, private sidings and the railway company.

Fans: Usually described as back or front fans, groups of sidings connected to a **gathering line.**

Fly shunting: Making a run with the engine in front of the wagons and uncoupling the latter while in motion, then accelerating to allow the following wagon(s) to be diverted into a siding after the engine has passed over the entry points. Fly shunting was prohibited except when there was no other reasonably practicable means of performing the work.

Gathering line: A line connecting the shunting line at the arrival or departure end of sidings.

Head shunt: Alternative description for **shunting line**.

'Hit 'em up': From shunter to driver: accelerate quickly so that the buffers will compress fully to aid uncoupling and give momentum to the wagon(s) afterward (especially if the wagon has some distance to travel down the yard to stop your engine).

Inside, or **inside clear:** Not obstructing any running line or sidings.

Knob up: Change or set the points to allow wagons to run in a particular direction.

Loading gauge: A gauge that set the maximum dimensions for locomotives, rolling stock and any loaded wagon to travel over a particular line.

Marshalling: (A) The movement of locomotives and/or rolling stock from where they satnd to where they are required to be. (B) A schedule showing the composition of either passenger or freight trains.

Marshalling yard: Sidings where incoming wagons were received, examined and made up by shunting into trains ('sorted' is another term that was used), to be worked forward to their next destination. The sidings in the yard were usually dedicated to traffic for specific destinations. No loading or unloading took place at these sidings.

Mileage sidings: Sidings in a station yard for traffic charged on a purely mileage basis – i.e. when the railway was not involved in collecting or delivering the goods. An example was coal loaded by the colliery and unloaded by a coal merchant. **Public siding** is another description for a similar arrangement.

On the engine: The practice of shunting when one or more vehicles are being propelled and others pulled. Also used to describe vehicles coupled immediately behind the engine.

Originating point: Where traffic commences its journey.

Private sidings: Connected to but not owned by a railway company. They could be colliery sidings, steel, gas or electricity works, or other large industrial companies. Alternatively, the term can denote quite a simple affair of just one or two sidings.

Public sidings: Where traffic (often coal) could either be loaded or unloaded in the open and did not have to go into a goods shed. Sometimes referred to as wharfs.

Reception sidings: For incoming traffic.

Rough shunt: When wagons have been allowed to crash into each other while shunting was taking place.

Roughs, or rough order: Wagons that have been shunted into line order but not station order.

Section order: See **Station order**.

Set: See **Dress the siding**.

Shunt: The movement of locomotives and/or rolling stock from where they stand to where they are required to be.

Shunting line: A line from where wagons were pushed/propelled forward into designated sidings, clear of the running lines.

Shunting neck: Alternative description for **shunting line**.

Sorted: Alternative description for the completing the process of **shunting**.

Sorting sidings: Where wagons were placed after they had been shunted to make up trains.

Station order: A goods train marshalled so that all the wagons for the same station are coupled together as a group and assembled in an order conducive to easy shunting at successive stations. (Note that this does not necessarily mean the wagons were sorted into the sequential order of the stations at which the train would arrive. A group of wagons for a station with sidings facing the train might be placed at the rear to enable easy access, once the engine had run around its train to shunt the sidings.)

Stowage sidings: Usually found at a marshalling yard; used to stow wagons that were not currently required for traffic purposes.

Terminating point: The opposite of **originating point**, this is where consigned traffic journeys end.

Tow-roping: The movement of vehicles by towing with a rope attached to the engine.

Traffic sidings: Another term for sidings within a goods or **marshalling yard**.

Trap points: Installed at the entry to a running line from sidings and under the control of the signalman, to prevent an engine or vehicle running onto the main line without authority.

Yard: This term has a variety of meanings: (A) station yard or station limits, the area inside the outermost home signal and starting signal – station yard could also describe sidings close to a passenger station; (B) sidings that are part of a larger area, e.g. 'top yard' or 'bottom yard'; (C) goods yard sidings that may include a goods shed, usually but not always close to a passenger station; (D) sometimes used as an abbreviation for **marshalling yard**; (E) almost any collection of sidings.

Other railway terms not directly related to shunting that do not appear in *Railway Operation for the Modeller*

Catch points: Positioned on steep gradients to deliberately derail trains running away in the wrong direction. They were also used on the entry line to goods lines or sidings where there was a connection to passenger lines. They were normally open to the reverse direction.

Cess: The narrow shoulder of the track formation beyond the ballast outside the running line. A preferred walking route.

Ease up: To move back onto the train, compressing the buffers in order to slacken them.

Flagman: A man equipped with flags, hand lamps and detonators to protect men working on the lines, authorised to stop trains if necessary.

Fog signalman: A man equipped with flags, hand lamps and detonators appointed to protect trains during fog and falling snow, stationed at distant signals.

Four foot: The term for the area between the running rails (4ft 8½in).

Lookout man: Appointed to act as lookout when men were working on or adjacent to the running lines, equipped with a horn or whistle, flags and detonators.

On the block: One train standing at stop signals at a signalbox with another train behind standing at the next stop signal, and so on. It can also relate to trains standing one behind the other on certain goods lines where this was permitted.

Six foot: The term for the area between two parallel running lines (normally 6ft 5½in).

Wide way: The area between a main line and parallel goods line or a siding greater than 6ft 5½in; a width which affords a safe space for railwaymen.

Wipper in: A train that conveys traffic to a particular destination; usually used to describe the last train of the day or week from point A to point B.

Select bibliography

British Railway Behind the Scenes, A. J. W. Williamson B.Sc, Ernest Benn Ltd, 1933

Freight Train Operation for the Railway Modeller, R. J. Essery, Ian Allan Publishing, 2005

General Directions to Agents and Members of Their Staffs, Management of Stations and Conveyance of Merchandise Traffic, LMS document, 1936

GWR General Appendix to the Rule Book, 1936

GWR Goods Services: Goods Depots and Their Operation Part 2A/2B, Tony Atkins, Wild Swan Publications Ltd, 2009/10

Illustrated History of the Ashchurch to Barnt Green Line, An, R. J. Essery, OPC, 2002

Midland Record 4, Wild Swan Publications Ltd, contains a detailed description of the work of a goods guard, 1996

Midland Record 13, Wild Swan Publications Ltd, contains an article about 'Hand Shunting Signals at Mantle Lane Sidings', 2000

Midland Record 23, Wild Swan Publications Ltd, contains an article about the Longbridge and Halesowen Joint Line, 2006

Midland Record 26, Wild Swan Publications Ltd, contains a detailed description of Washwood Heath Marshalling Yard, 2008

Outline of Railway Traffic Operation, An, T. F. Cameron, Railway Publishing Company, 1946

Passenger Train Operation for the Railway Modeller, R. J. Essery, Ian Allan Publishing, 2005

Railway Operating Statistics, C. Mossop, The Railway Gazette, 1911

Railway Operation for the Modeller, R. J. Essery, Ian Allan Publishing, 2003

Railway Goods Station, The, Fred. W. West, E. & F. Spon Ltd, 1912

Railway Permanent Way, William Heyworth and J. Thomas Lee, Charles Sever, 1922

Railway Signalling and Track Plans, R. J. Essery, Ian Allan Publishing, 2007

Railways of England, W. M. Ackworth, John Murray 1889, reprinted, Ian Allan Publishing

Shunter's Manual, The, Edward S. Hadley, published by the author, 1944

Working and Management of an English Railway, The, George Findlay, Whittaker & Co, 1890